A Country Store In Your Mailbox®

Holidays at Home

A Country Store In Your Mailbox®

Gooseberry Patch
149 Johnson Drive
Department BOOK
Delaware, OH 43015
★
1·800·85·GOOSE
1-800·854·6673

Copyright 1998, Gooseberry Patch® 1-888052-26-0
Third Printing, June, 1999

All rights reserved. No part of this book may be reproduced or utilized in any form or by any means, electronic or mechanical, including photocopying and recording, or by any information storage and retrieval system, without permission in writing from the publisher.

How To Subscribe

Would you like to receive
"A Country Store in Your Mailbox"®?
For a 2-year subscription to our 88-page
Gooseberry Patch catalog, simply send $3.00 to:

Gooseberry Patch
149 Johnson Drive
Department BOOK
Delaware, OH 43015

Contents...

To everyone who finds joy in a harvest moon, a fresh blanket of snow, twinkling tree lights and Christmas carols, this book is for you!

APPRECIATION

Our heartfelt thanks to all our Gooseberry Patch friends for sharing tender moments, magical memories and treasured holiday traditions...

The Harvest Kitchen

Garlic Chicken Wings

Eileen Watts
East Brunswick, NJ

Serve with crusty French or Italian bread!

18 chicken wings, cut in half
minced garlic to taste
fresh parsley
oregano
salt
pepper
Parmesan cheese
1/2 c. red wine vinegar

Place chicken wings in shallow baking pan. Sprinkle garlic, parsley, oregano, salt, pepper and cheese to taste over wings. Bake 350 degrees for one hour. Remove pan from oven, pour red wine vinegar over wings and bake another 5 to 10 minutes. Serves 2 for dinner, or makes a great appetizer.

Send out invitations for an autumn get-together! Keep the food simple...hot dogs for grilling, potato salad, baked beans, chips, veggies and fruit. After a moonlight hayride, enjoy S'mores by a toasty bonfire!

Barbeque Spareribs

Sammy Elann Morrison
Aurora, CO

These are mouth-watering!

1-1/2 lbs. spareribs
1 lemon, sliced
1 onion, sliced
3/4 c. catsup
1-1/2 t. salt
1/4 c. vinegar
1 c. water
2 T. Worcestershire sauce
1/4 c. sugar

Lay ribs, meaty side up in a shallow roasting pan. Place a slice of lemon and onion on each. Roast at 450 degrees oven for 30 minutes. In a saucepan combine catsup, salt, vinegar, water, Worcestershire sauce and sugar; bring all to a boil. After ribs have cooked 30 minutes in oven, add sauce and continue baking in oven one hour at 350 degrees. Baste ribs with sauce every 15 minutes. If sauce thickens, add more water.

Don't put your grill away when summer's over! Fall can be the greatest time of the year for cookouts...the bugs are gone and the cooler weather makes for perfect outdoor suppers!

Carolyn Gulley
Cumberland Gap, TN

Fabulous Fajitas

Sharon Pruess
South Ogden, UT

So versatile and delicious!

1 lb. skinless chicken breast, cut into strips
2 T. cornstarch
2 T. lemon juice
1 t. garlic powder
1 t. seasoned salt
1/2 t. pepper
1/2 t. oregano
1/8 t. liquid smoke flavoring
2 T. oil
1 c. green bell pepper strips
1 c. onion wedges, thinly sliced
1 c. tomato wedges, thinly sliced
1/2 c. salsa
warmed flour tortillas
sour cream

In medium bowl, combine first 8 ingredients. Cover and refrigerate 2 to 8 hours to marinate. Discard marinade. In a skillet, heat oil until very hot. Sauté chicken until just cooked. Add green pepper and onion; continue cooking until crisp-tender. Add tomato and salsa; simmer one minute longer. Serve immediately in tortillas, top with additional salsa and sour cream. You can also substitute one pound of beef steak, cut across grain in 1/4-inch strips, or raw shrimp, peeled and deveined.

Indian corn hung in a cluster with dried statice, yarrow and bittersweet tied with a raffia bow makes a stunning autumn display. Best of all, when you replace it with Christmas wreaths, the birds and squirrels will love the Indian corn treat!

Mary Rose Kulczak, Temperance, MI

Tortilla Black Bean Casserole

Kathy Grashoff
Ft. Wayne, IN

Terrific with Spanish rice and a salad!

2 c. chopped onion
1-1/2 c. green pepper, chopped
14-1/2 oz. can tomatoes, chopped
3/4 c. picante sauce
2 cloves garlic, minced
2 t. ground cumin
15-oz. can black beans or red kidney beans, drained
12 6-inch corn tortillas
2 c. fat-free Monterey Jack cheese, shredded

In a large skillet, combine onion, green pepper, undrained tomatoes, picante sauce, garlic and cumin. Bring to boiling; reduce heat. Simmer uncovered, for 10 minutes. Stir in beans. Spread one-third of the bean mixture over bottom of a 13"x9" pan. Top with half of the tortillas, overlapping as necessary, and half of cheese. Add another third of the bean mixture, then remaining tortillas and bean mixture. Cover and bake in a 350 degree oven for 30 to 35 minutes, or until heated through. Sprinkle with remaining cheese. Let stand for 10 minutes. Cut into squares to serve. Makes 10 to12 side servings or 6 to 8 main dish servings.

Save cornstalks from your garden and tie them to your lamp post or front porch posts. Thread golden or amber Christmas lights through the stalks to brighten your entrance during the harvest season!

Marjorie Jergesen, Erie, PA

Herbed Snap Bean Salad

Mary Dungan
Gardenville, PA

Use beans from your garden when you can.

4 c. snap beans,
  sliced and cooked
1 med. red onion, thinly sliced
1/2 c. bell pepper, diced
1/2 c. celery, diced
1/8 t. dried oregano
1/2 t. dried dill weed
1/2 t. salt
1/4 t. black pepper
1 lg. clove garlic, minced
1/3 c. oil
1/4 c. cider vinegar
1/4 c. red wine
1/4 c. sugar

Cook snap beans 7 minutes and plunge in ice water to stop cooking. Add onion, bell pepper, and celery in a large bowl with beans. Shake remaining ingredients together in jar, pour over salad and chill 2 to 24 hours, stirring several times.

Dress up a wheelbarrow! Line it with a colorful plastic tablecloth before filling it with ice and beverage cans, then use it as an outdoor party cooler.

Wanda Wood, Loudon, TN

Molly's Five Bean Bake

Mary Young Jackson
Flower Mound, TX

So easy to make!

1 lb. 15-oz. can pork and beans
15-oz. can barbecued beans
15-oz. can kidney beans
15-oz. can butter beans
15-oz. can white beans
1 lb. center cut bacon, cut in
  1-inch pieces
3/4 c. brown sugar
1/2 c. white vinegar
1/2 c. onion, chopped
1 t. dry mustard
1 t. garlic salt

Partially drain beans then combine all ingredients in 3-1/2 quart casserole. Bake uncovered, at 350 degrees, 2-1/2 hours. Makes approximately 20 servings, leftovers can be frozen.

Don't forget our feathered friends as the weather turns cooler. It's a breeze to fill bird feeders if you remove the spray cap from a garden watering can. The spout fits into feeders with small openings, and the seed pours out easily!

Pat Habiger
Spearville, KS

Black Bean Chili

Vickie

A family favorite!

1 lb. dried black beans
1 lb. ground beef
2 T. canola oil
1 lg. onion, chopped
3 cloves garlic, crushed
3 T. chili powder
1 T. whole cumin seeds
1 T. Worcestershire sauce
28-oz. can tomatoes, pureéd
1 bell pepper, chopped

Place black beans in a stockpot, cover with water and let soak overnight. When ready to cook, drain water from beans and cover with fresh water. Simmer until tender, approximately one to 2 hours. Brown the ground beef in oil, adding onion, garlic and chili powder. Drain fat and add remaining ingredients, including beans. Simmer for one hour, or until beans are very tender.

"We have had our summer evenings, now for our October eves!"

-Humbert Wolfe

Nana's Refrigerator Pickles

Jeanne Calkins
Midland, Michigan

A delicious, no-fuss recipe!

7 c. small cucumbers, thinly sliced
1 c. onions, thinly sliced
1 c. green bell pepper, thinly sliced
2 T. coarse salt
2 t. celery seed
2 c. white vinegar
1 c. sugar

Place vegetables in a colander and sprinkle with salt. Let sit 15 minutes to drain. Mix the celery seed, vinegar and sugar until sugar is dissolved. Pack vegetables in quart jars, then pour syrup mixture over vegetables. Wipe off rim of jars and place a piece of plastic wrap over jar mouth. Add the lid and ring on each jar. Store in the refrigerator at least one week before serving. Keeps up to 6 months when refrigerated.

I love to hang bittersweet from my kitchen and dining area curtains. I also drape long sprays across my mantle.

Carol Atwood, Bristol, CT

Pumpkin Bars

Kathy Grashoff
Ft. Wayne, IN

Perfect for autumn!

1 c. flour
2/3 c. sugar
1 t. baking powder
1 t. ground cinnamon
1/2 t. baking soda
1/8 t. salt
1/8 t. ground cloves
1 c. canned pumpkin
2 egg whites, slightly beaten
1/4 c. oil
1/4 c. water

Spray 17"x11-1/2" baking pan with nonstick coating; set pan aside. In medium mixing bowl, combine flour, sugar, baking powder, cinnamon, baking soda, salt and cloves. Stir in pumpkin, egg whites, oil and water until thoroughly combined. Spread batter into the pan. Bake at 350 degrees for 20 to 25 minutes, until toothpick inserted near center comes out clean. Cool in pan on a wire rack, frost. Cut into 24 bars. Cover and store in refrigerator.

Frosting:

1/4 c. light cream cheese
1-3/4 c. powdered sugar
1 t. vanilla
1/4 t. grated lemon or orange peel

In medium bowl, beat together cream cheese, one cup powdered sugar, vanilla and grated lemon or orange peel, until mixture is light and fluffy. Gradually beat in remaining powdered sugar

Winona's Lemon Whippersnappers

Mel Wolk
St. Peters, MO

These have a nice lemon flavor and are so easy to make!

1 pkg. lemon cake mix
2 c. frozen whipped topping, thawed
1 egg
1/2 c. powdered sugar, sifted

Grease cookie sheets. Combine cake mix, whipped topping and egg in large bowl and stir until well mixed. Drop by teaspoon into powdered sugar and roll to coat. Bake at 350 degrees for 10 to 15 minutes until golden brown. Remove from cookie sheet and cool. Makes 4 dozen cookies.

I like to fill antique canning jars with cranberries to add a harvest feel to my kitchen decor.

LuElla Reimer, Hillsboro, KS

Indian Summer Chicken Casserole

Dee Rogers
South Charleston, WV

This easy casserole can be prepared ahead and frozen.

3 or 4 large chicken breasts, cooked and deboned
2 10-oz. cans cream of celery soup
1 stick margarine
1/2 c. onion, chopped
1/2 c. celery, chopped
1 pkg. herb seasoned stuffing mix
1 c. milk

After stewing chicken and deboning, put in 13"x9" pan; reserve broth. On top of chicken, spread undiluted cream of celery soup. Add one cup of the reserved chicken broth to a saucepan and add margarine. Mix in the onion and celery and cook until tender. Add the stuffing to the onion mixture, mix gently and spread over the soup and chicken. Pour milk over all and bake in 350 degree oven for 30 minutes. Serves 8 to 10.

Host an old-fashioned barn dance! If you know someone who plays a banjo or fiddle, invite them to come along! Enjoy some long forgotten dance steps and lots of good food. Have plenty of icy cold cider to quench thirsty guests!

Pork Barbecue Sandwiches

Ann Rudnicki
Riverside, Ohio

My mother has made this recipe for over 40 years!

2 T. vinegar
20-oz. bottle of catsup
1 T. mustard
1 T. Worcestershire sauce
salt & pepper to taste
3 T. brown sugar
1 med. onion, chopped
1/2 c. celery, chopped
1 T. oil
3 lbs. pork, cooked and shredded

Mix the first 10 ingredients in skillet and simmer for 15 to 20 minutes. Add the shredded meat and heat thoroughly.

Take time to do special autumn crafts with your children...preserving autumn leaves, carving pumpkins, baking cookies, or making a family scarecrow. Invite their friends or neighborhood kids to share in the fun. It will create a special memory for all.

Marion Pfeifer, Smyrna, DE

Autumn Red Potato Casserole

Pam Hilton
Centerburg, OH

This will be a favorite in your family!

8 med. red potatoes
3 c. mild Cheddar cheese
1/4 c. butter
1 pt. sour cream
1/3 c. green onions, chopped
1/4 t. salt
1 t. pepper

Boil potatoes until tender, but firm. Allow potatoes to cool, then peel and dice. In a heavy saucepan, combine cheese and butter over low heat. Stir until cheese melts. Remove from heat and blend in sour cream, onions, salt and pepper. Pour over potatoes and gently fold in. Transfer potatoes into a casserole dish, dot with butter and bake at 350 degrees for 30 to 40 minutes.

On a cool evening, invite friends over to enjoy a crackling fire, warm apple cider and a favorite movie.

Apple Orchard Green Beans

JoAnn

A terrific way to use the last beans from your summer garden.

2 c. fresh green beans, cut into 2-inch pieces
1 c. carrots, sliced thin
2 green onions, chopped
1/2 c. water
1 t. sugar
1/4 t. dried thyme, crushed
1/3 c. apple juice
1 t. cornstarch
1/2 c. Red Delicious apple, chopped

Combine green beans, carrots, onions, water, sugar and thyme in a large saucepan. Bring to a boil, then reduce heat to low. Cover and simmer until vegetables are crisp-tender, approximately 5 minutes. Pour apple juice into a small mixing bowl, blend in cornstarch, stirring until dissolved. Add to vegetables, stir, add apple. Continue to simmer on low for 2 minutes until sauce has thickened. Serves 6.

Autumn garden tips: By the end of November cut your peony stems back to the ground, and begin planting crocus, daffodils and tulips to brighten your garden next spring!

Harvest Time Potatoes

Carol Bull
Gooseberry Patch

So cheesy!

3-1/2 lbs. baking potatoes
salt and pepper to taste
3/4 T. dried thyme
3 c. Havarti, Monterey Jack, or white Cheddar cheese, shredded
3 T. flour
1-1/3 c. cream
1-1/3 c. chicken stock
1/4 c. Dijon mustard

Preheat oven to 400 degrees. Spray large casserole with non-stick cooking spray. Peel potatoes and slice 1/8 inch thick. Arrange one third of the potatoes in the dish. Sprinkle with salt and pepper. Add one third of the thyme, one-third of the cheese and one tablespoon of flour. Continue adding 2 more layers of potatoes, seasonings, flour and cheese. Combine the cream, chicken stock and mustard in bowl. Pour over the potatoes. Bake 50 to 60 minutes or until the top is golden and crusty and potatoes are tender. Makes 8 servings.

Create a clever harvest decoration for your porch! Fill a large terra cotta pot with mini pumpkins then nestle a smaller pot inside among the pumpkins. Fill this pot with pretty red apples. Set a small pot in among the apples and place a pillar candle inside. Beautiful!

Tomato Basil Soup

Kristi Hartland
State College, PA

Wonderful on a cool autumn day.

1-1/2 c. Vidalia onions, diced
10 basil leaves, chopped
2 T. garlic, chopped
28-oz. can whole tomatoes
2 28-oz. cans diced
    plum tomatoes
1/8 c. sugar
salt
ground pepper
red pepper flakes
2 c. skim milk or cream

Sauté onions, basil and garlic in a pan sprayed with non-stick vegetable spray. Process whole tomatoes in blender or food processor for 10 seconds; set aside. When onions are soft, add tomatoes and sugar, simmer on low for 2 hours. Season with salt, pepper and red pepper flakes to taste. Add skim milk or cream, and heat through. Vary the taste by adding a cup of frozen chopped spinach, thawed and drained, to the onions and sauté, or add 1/2 cup mozzarella cheese to a bowl before adding soup. Top with garlic croutons.

Search out farmer's markets and purchase dried flowers, bittersweet, lemon leaves and wheat to create your own harvest bouquet. Making your own is easy and relaxing! Spend a quiet Sunday afternoon tucking your treasures in a basket and place it somewhere you'll see it often to enjoy it through the season. A reminder of the simple beauty of nature.

Jack-o'-Lantern Stew

Mel Wolk
St. Peters, MO

A wonderful beef barley soup served in a hollowed-out pumpkin!

1 lb. ground chuck
1 T. vegetable oil
2 T. flour
4 c. beef broth or bouillon
16-oz. can tomatoes
1/4 c. pearled barley
1/3 c. onion, chopped
2 carrots, peeled and chopped
1 rib celery, chopped
salt and black pepper to taste

Cook beef in oil in large saucepan for about 5 minutes or until it loses its red color. Stir occasionally to break up large chunks of meat. Sprinkle flour over beef and stir until flour loses its white color. Slowly add broth, stirring constantly. Peel and chop tomatoes, reserving juice. Add tomatoes and juice to beef mixture, with remaining ingredients and bring to boil. Reduce heat and simmer, stirring occasionally, until barley and vegetables are tender, about 60 minutes. Cut the top off of a medium pumpkin and scoop out the seeds, cleaning well. Add hot soup, replace pumpkin top and serve. You can even add more autumn fun by serving the soup in small Jack-be-Little pumpkins...they make perfect bowls! Makes 4 to 6 servings.

You'll need to begin forcing bulbs by November 15th if you plan to give them as holiday gifts.

Crunchy Granny Smith Salad

Gloria Kaufmann
Orrville, OH

A refreshing combination!

1 lg. head red leaf lettuce, torn
2 Granny Smith apples, sliced and cut in half
4 oz. Swiss cheese, grated
4 oz. cashews, chopped
1 c. oil
1 T. onion, minced
1 t. dry mustard
1/2 c. sugar
1/3 c. vinegar
2 t. poppy seed

Layer the first 4 ingredients in bowl. Mix the remaining ingredients in blender for poppy seed dressing. Pour dressing over salad.

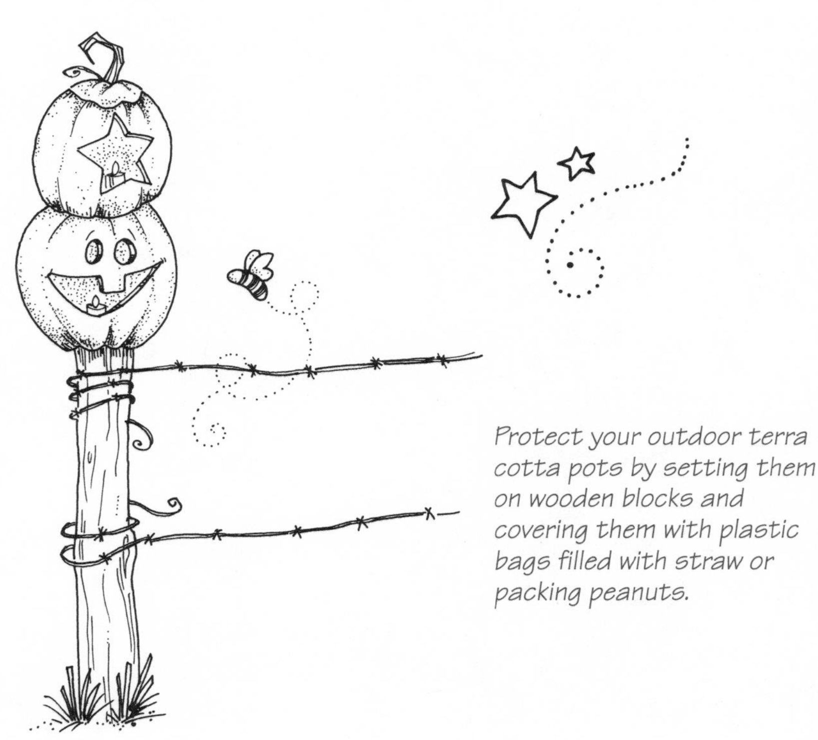

Protect your outdoor terra cotta pots by setting them on wooden blocks and covering them with plastic bags filled with straw or packing peanuts.

Country Beer Bread

Wendy Lee Paffenroth
Pine Island, NY

This bread freezes well for up to one month.

3 c. flour
3 T sugar
1 T. baking powder
1 t. salt
12 oz. beer, room temperature

Preheat oven to 375 degrees. Oil a 9"x5" loaf pan. In large bowl combine dry ingredients. Add beer all at once and stir with a wooden spoon, mixture will be very sticky. Put in loaf pan and bake at 375 degrees for 35 to 45 minutes. Cool on rack.

This year make a "snowman" style scarecrow! Stack 3 pumpkins together using sticks and branches for his arms. Surround him with bales of hay and lots of autumn leaves, cornshocks and Indian corn!

Sherian Oakely, Tullahoma, TN

Slow Cooker Apple Butter

Michelle Maris
Lincoln, IL

Try this apple butter on pancakes, too!

4 lb. apples, stemmed and quartered
1 c. apple cider
2-1/2 c. sugar
1 t. cinnamon
1 t. cloves
1/2 t. allspice

Cook the apples and cider in a slow cooker 10 hours or overnight on high. Sift the apples through a food mill and return pulp to the slow cooker. Add the balance of the ingredients and cook one hour longer. You may want to leave lid off slow cooker to cook off some liquid. Ladle into hot, sterilized pint jars, leaving 1/4-inch headspace. Process in a boiling water canner for 10 minutes.

As the temperature drops, animals need warm, cozy places to sleep too! If you have outdoor dogs or barn cats, make sure you have plenty of straw beds for them to snuggle down into, along with lots of fresh water and food.

Glazed Apple Pie Bars

Margaret Scoresby
Mount Vernon, OH

These won't last long!

2-1/2 c. flour
1 c. shortening
2 T. sugar
1 t. salt
1 egg, separated
2/3 c. milk
2 21-oz. cans apple pie filling
2 T. butter
1/3 c. brown sugar
1-1/2 c. powdered sugar
2 T. milk
3 T. butter, melted

Combine flour, shortening, sugar and salt with a fork or pastry blender. Blend egg yolk and milk well, stir into flour mixture. Roll half of dough on a floured board until large enough to fit into a jelly roll pan, then place in pan. Spoon pie filling over dough, dot with butter and sprinkle with brown sugar. Roll out remaining dough large enough to cover filling, then seal edges of dough. Beat egg white until frothy and brush over crust. Bake at 375 degrees for 35 to 45 minutes. Combine remaining ingredients and glaze warm apple pie bars.

Turn mini pumpkins into candle holders by cutting out the center and placing a taper inside. Candles in terra cotta pots also add to the natural look of harvest-time.

Tina Empey, Provo, UT

Chocolate Spice Cake

Judy Kelly
St. Charles, MO

A delicious cake!

1 box German chocolate cake mix
1-1/2 t. cinnamon
3 eggs, slightly beaten
1 can raisin pie filling

Mix cake mix and cinnamon. Add eggs and pie filling. Stir just until dry ingredients are moistened. Put in a greased tube or Bundt® pan. Bake at 350 degrees for 55 minutes to one hour. Let cool before removing from pan.

Autumn is a fun time to decorate! Line a collection of witches on your mantel. Create trees by adding some bare branches from your yard, place gourds, leaves and bittersweet between the witches and trees. At Thanksgiving replace the witches with turkeys or Pilgrims.

Marion Pfeifer, Smyrna, DE

Maple-Glazed Ribs

Sandra Nichols
Summerfield, IL

A mouth-watering harvest meal!

3 lbs. pork spareribs, cut into serving-size pieces
1 c. maple syrup
3 T. orange juice concentrate
2 T. soy sauce
1 T. Dijon mustard
1 T. Worcestershire sauce
1 t. curry powder
1 clove garlic, minced
2 green onions, minced
3 T. catsup
1 T. sesame seeds, toasted

Place ribs, meaty side up, on a rack in a greased 13"x9"x2" baking pan. Cover pan tightly with foil. Bake at 350 degrees for 1-1/4 hours. Meanwhile, combine the next 9 ingredients in a saucepan. Bring to a boil over medium heat. Reduce heat; simmer for 15 minutes, stirring occasionally. Drain ribs; remove rack and return ribs to pan. Cover with sauce. Bake, uncovered, for 25 minutes, basting occasionally. Sprinkle with sesame seeds just before serving. Serves 6.

Grow a bittersweet plant in your backyard...they vine beautifully and all fall and winter you will have sprigs of bittersweet berries for arrangement and wreaths.

Twila Robinson, Rock Island, IL

Vermont Chicken With Apples

The Governor's Inn
Ludlow, VT

Garnish with fresh parsley.

4 med. boneless chicken breasts, cut in half
1 T. olive oil
1 T. sweet unsalted butter
1/3 c. shallots, chopped
1/4 c. apple brandy
1/4 t. thyme
1/4 t. salt
1/4 t. freshly cracked pepper
3/4 c. apple juice
2 Granny Smith apples, halved, cored and sliced
3/4 c. heavy cream

In large sauté pan, brown chicken in oil and butter mixture. Drain off all but one tablespoon of drippings for pan. Add shallots and sauté until soft, scraping up some of the browned bits in the sauté pan. Return chicken to sauté pan, pour on apple brandy. Carefully ignite and let flame die down. Sprinkle chicken with thyme, salt and half of the pepper. Pour the apple juice over chicken and bring to a boil. Lower heat and simmer covered for 20 minutes. Remove cover, place apples over top of chicken, re-cover and cook 10 minutes longer. Chicken temperature should read 160 degrees and apples should be tender. With slotted spoon remove chicken and apples to a serving platter; keep warm. Pour pan drippings into a glass measuring cup. Allow to stand a few minutes for fat to rise to the top; remove fat. Return juices to sauté pan; bring quickly to boil and reduce by almost half. Sauce will begin to look like syrup. Stir in cream and heat until sauce starts to thicken. Spoon over chicken and apples. Serves 4.

Country Fresh Green Beans

Michelle Parkinson
Vernal, UT

Even the kids will love this!

1-1/2 c. fresh green beans
8 slices bacon
8 fresh new red potatoes, sliced
1/2 c. sweet onion, chopped
salt and pepper to taste
1 c. mild Cheddar cheese, grated
2 tomatoes, chopped

Cook green beans in water until crisp-tender. Drain and set aside. Cook the bacon, drain and crumble. Set aside reserving grease. Fry potatoes in bacon grease along with the sweet onion. Season with pepper and seasoned salt of your choice. When almost done, add the green beans and bacon to warm them and finish cooking potatoes until tender. When done, top with Cheddar cheese and tomatoes. Let cheese melt before serving.

Host a wreath party! Invite several friends over and have each one bring a grapevine wreath and one or two decorative items such as silk fall flowers, pine cones, acorns, bows, leaves, bittersweet, raffia and a glue gun. Spend a few hours creating beautiful autumn wreaths while sipping cider and enjoying good company.

Valerie Boersma, Alfred, NY

Sweet Potato Bake

Kim Henry
Library, PA

Everyone will want second helpings!

3 c. yams
1/2 c. sugar
1 t. vanilla
1/2 c. milk
1/4 c. butter or margarine
2 eggs

Cook potatoes with skins, then peel and mash. Mix well with the remaining ingredients. Pour into a 13"x9" dish. Add topping.

Topping:

1/2 c. flour
3/4 c. brown sugar
1/2 c. butter, melted
1/2 c. pecans, chopped

Combine all ingredients well and sprinkle over sweet potatoes. Bake at 325 degrees for one hour. Serves 10 to 12.

"Sing a song of seasons! Something bright in all! Flowers in the summer, Fires in the fall!"

-Robert Louis Stevenson

Corn-Cheddar Chowder

Robbi Courtaway
St. Louis, MO

Combine this hearty soup with homemade biscuits.

3 T. margarine
1 lg. onion, chopped
2 vegetable or chicken bouillon cubes
1 T. flour
2 t. dry mustard
1/4 t. cayenne pepper
1-1/2 t. dried thyme
6 med. potatoes, peeled and diced
16 oz. frozen corn
2 c. half-and-half
1 c. milk
2 c. Cheddar cheese, shredded
1/2 t. celery salt

In large, heavy saucepan, melt margarine. Add onion and cook 8 or 9 minutes, until softened. Dissolve bouillon in 2-1/2 cups of boiling water; set aside. Combine flour, mustard, cayenne pepper and thyme in small container, add to saucepan and cook over low heat another 2 minutes, stirring constantly. Stir in bouillon mixture and bring to a simmer. Add potatoes and cook, covered, over low heat, approximately 20 minutes, until tender. Add the corn, half-and-half and milk and bring to a simmer. Remove pan from heat and stir in shredded cheese and celery salt, stirring until thoroughly combined. Serves 4.

Gather together your family and take a Sunday drive in the country! Pack a picnic, take a walk, linger as long as you can to enjoy the beautiful colors around you!

Creamy Butternut Soup

Jo Ann

Warm and comforting.

- 5 lbs. butternut squash, peeled and chopped
- 1-1/2 lbs. Red Delicious apples, quartered
- 1" cinnamon stick
- 2 qts. chicken stock
- 3 sticks butter
- 1/3 c. maple syrup
- 1/2 t. nutmeg
- 1 pt. light cream

Steam squash, apples and cinnamon stick together until squash is tender. Remove cinnamon stick and place remaining mixture through a food mill. Add to a large saucepan. Stir in chicken stock, butter, syrup and nutmeg; simmer 15 minutes. In a small saucepan, heat cream until hot, but not boiling. Add to soup mixture and stir well. Serves 8.

Open a white Lumina pumpkin from the bottom and thoroughly clean out the inside. Use moon and star cookie cutters as tracing guides for cutting out designs all over your pumpkin. Set your harvest pumpkin over a votive candle... a great centerpiece!

Beth Haney
Edwards, IL

Sour Cream Cornbread

Cathy Hurley
Poca, WV

Easy to make!

1 c. self-rising cornmeal
8-oz. carton sour cream
3 lg. eggs, lightly beaten
1/4 c. vegetable oil

Heat a lightly greased 8" cast-iron skillet, or deep dish pie pan in a 400 degree oven for 5 minutes. Combine cornmeal and remaining ingredients, stirring just until moistened. Remove prepared skillet from oven, and spoon batter into skillet. Bake at 400 degrees for 30 minutes or until golden. Serves 4 to 6.

Make arrangements of dried materials in old crocks or churns. I use bittersweet, yarrow, sunflowers and wheat. I also let ivy trail down. An old molasses can to hold your arrangement gives a really primitive look.

Sherian Oakley, Tullahoma, TN

Parsley Biscuits

Jo Ann

Enjoy these warm from the oven.

2 c. all-purpose flour
1/2 t. salt
1 T. baking powder
zest of one lemon
3 T. fresh parsley, chopped
1/2 c. vegetable shortening
1/2 c. milk
1/4 c. heavy cream

In a large mixing bowl, combine flour, salt, baking powder, lemon zest and parsley. Using a pastry cutter or two knives, cut in shortening until mixture resembles oatmeal. Add milk and cream, blend until mixture forms a ball. Place dough on a lightly floured surface and knead 5 times. Roll out dough to 1/2-inch thickness and cut biscuits. Place on lightly oiled baking sheets and bake at 425 degrees for 15 minutes or until golden. Makes 20 to 24 biscuits.

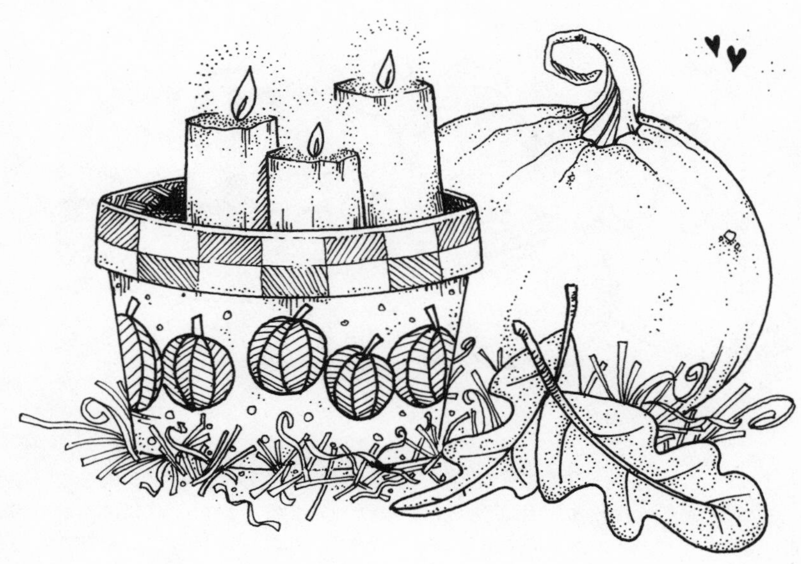

Fill antique canning jars with candy corn and tuck them in your cupboard for a harvest display.

Jennifer Barr, Loganville, GA

Sour Cream Apple Pie

Betty McKay
Harmony, MN

Enjoy this warm from the oven!

9-inch single pie crust
4 lg. apples, peeled and sliced
1/2 c. sugar
1/2 t. cinnamon
3 T. flour
16 oz. sour cream

Line pie tin with pie crust and flute the edges. Mix apples with sugar, cinnamon, flour and sour cream. Pour in pie crust. Bake for one hour at 375 degrees.

Decorate your front porch and mailbox with cornstalks, sprigs of bittersweet, Indian corn, pumpkins of all sizes, gourds and milo. Mix it all together for a great fall arrangement!

Stephanie McAtee, Kansas City, MO

Apple-Caramel Cake

Diane Harmon
Euclid, OH

Make this when the apples are fresh and abundant!

2 c sugar
1-1/2 c. oil
3 eggs
3 c. flour
2 t. cinnamon
1 t. baking soda
1/2 t. nutmeg
1/2 t. salt
2 t. vanilla
3 c. baking apples, pared, cored and diced
juice of one lemon
1 c. walnuts, chopped

In large bowl, combine sugar and oil. Beat until mixed. Add eggs, one at a time, beating well after each addition. Sift together flour, cinnamon, baking soda, nutmeg and salt. Add to egg mixture gradually, beating constantly. Add vanilla and combine thoroughly. Sprinkle apples with lemon juice and add to batter with walnuts (the batter will be very thick). Spoon into greased and floured Bundt® pan or large tube pan. Bake at 325 degrees for 75 minutes or until cake tests done. Remove from oven and cool in pan on wire rack for 15 minutes. Invert onto serving plate and cool completely on wire rack.

Caramel Glaze:

3 T. butter
3 T. brown sugar
2 T. milk
1/2 t. vanilla

In small saucepan, melt butter. Add brown sugar, milk and vanilla. Bring to a rolling boil and boil rapidly about 2 minutes. Cool slightly and spoon over cooled cake, allowing glaze to run down sides.

Old feed sacks filled with packing peanuts and tied with raffia, make great harvest decorations. Set them on your porch with bales of straw, pumpkins and a basket of gourds.

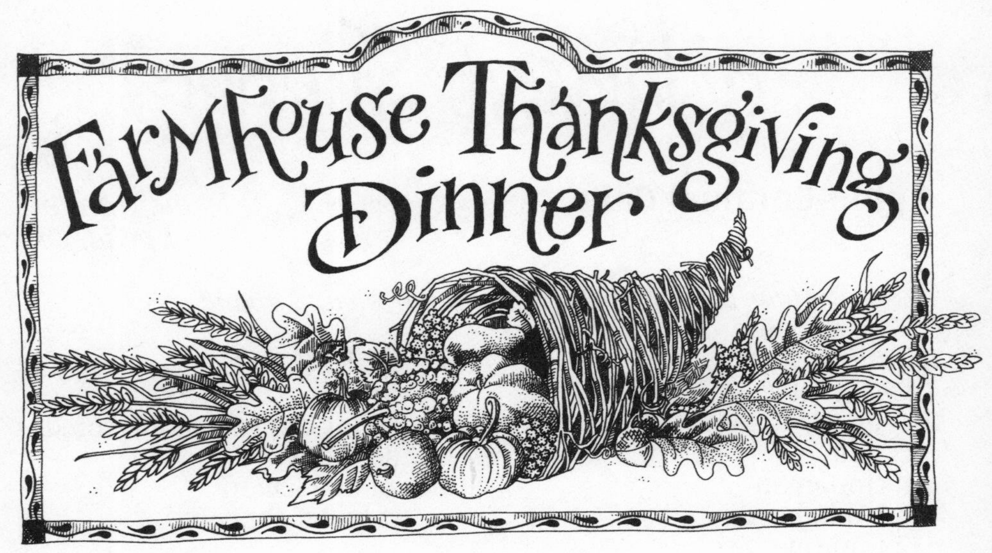

Turkey with Maple Glaze

Jo Ann Cain
Palmyra, IL

Leftovers make wonderful sandwiches!

12 to 16-lb. turkey
salt to taste
water
1 c. margarine, melted
pepper to taste
2/3 c. maple syrup

Wash turkey and pat dry. Sprinkle with salt. Put turkey in a large roaster, breast side down, in 2 inches of water. Add margarine and pepper. During the last half hour roasting, turn turkey breast side up, and brush with maple syrup. Allow turkey to brown.

Welcome your guests with a beautifully decorated door! Find some pretty twisting vines and hang them in a swag over and down the sides of your door. Wire gourds and Indian corn to a straw wreath; add a bunch of bittersweet tied with ribbon.

Farmhouse Thanksgiving Dinner

Fruited Pork Tenderloin

The Governor's Inn
Ludlow, VT

When the leaves begin to turn and the first fire is in the fireplace, this delicious recipe just seems to pop out of the recipe file!

1/2 c. dried apricots
2/3 c. apricot nectar
2 pork tenderloins, butterflied
12 pitted prunes
1 t. fresh ginger, minced
1/2 c. apricot preserves
1 t. soy sauce

Cook dried apricots in nectar for 4 minutes in a covered saucepan, reserve liquid. Let stand covered for an hour or overnight. Lay the two butterflied tenderloins open side up and place the drained apricots and prunes alternately over the tenderloins. Roll the meat around the fruits. Tie the 2 pieces of meat with cotton butcher string at 2-inch intervals. Rub the pork with fresh minced ginger. Place in a roasting pan and roast at 325 degrees until hand-held meat thermometer reaches 170 degrees. Brush pork occasionally during roasting with mixture of reserved liquid, apricot preserves and soy sauce. Remove string and slice. Serve on warm platter. Pour any juices around platter. Serves 6.

The day before Thanksgiving, take your children grocery shopping, letting them help you choose all the trimmings for a wonderful Thanksgiving meal. When you return home, fill a sturdy basket with all the food and deliver it to another family or a shelter. A wonderful teaching moment for children.

Apple & Sausage Stuffing

Carol Tomasetti-Records
Windham, CT

A favorite that your family will love.

1 lb. sweet Italian sausage
1 lg. onion, diced
2 stalks celery, chopped
1 apple, peeled, cored and diced
1 T. oil
2-1/2 c. water
1 stick margarine
1 lb. herb seasoned stuffing mix
1 t. fennel seeds

In a large skillet, brown sausage over medium heat. You may need to add a little oil if sausage is very lean. While browning, break sausage into pieces. Take sausage out of skillet with slotted spoon and place in large bowl. When cool, crumble into small pieces. Place onion, celery and apple with a tablespoon of oil in skillet. Sauté until tender. Remove from heat. Heat water and margarine to a boil. Remove from heat. In bowl, combine stuffing mix with water and margarine. Toss lightly until moist throughout. (You can add a little water if you prefer moister stuffing.) Add fennel seeds to stuffing mix, blend. Add stuffing and onion mixture to large bowl with sausage. Mix together thoroughly. Place stuffing in cavity of turkey or place in baking pan and bake at 350 degrees for 30 minutes. Serves 8 to 10.

Cornbread & Red Pepper Stuffing

Vickie

Terrific with any main dish!

8-1/2 oz. pkg. corn muffin mix
8 oz. bacon, cut into 2" pieces
1 lg. onion, chopped
1 lg. red bell pepper, chopped
3 c. unseasoned dry bread cubes
3 t. poultry seasoning
1/2 c. chicken broth
9-oz. pkg. frozen corn, thawed

Bake corn muffin mix according to package directions; cool then crumble. Fry bacon over medium heat until crisp. Remove from skillet and reserve drippings. Cook onion and red pepper in drippings until onion is transparent; stir occasionally. In a large bowl, gently combine crumbled corn bread, bread cubes, bacon and poultry seasoning. Add bell pepper and onion mixture, chicken broth and corn. Toss gently. If you are baking stuffing inside turkey, spoon loosely into neck and body cavity. Allow 1/2 cup of cornbread stuffing per pound of turkey. Stuffing can also be prepared in a slow cooker. Measure stuffing and spoon into slow cooker; cover. Set temperature to low setting. After 2 hours, add one tablespoon of chicken broth for each cup of stuffing in the slow cooker; gently mix. Continue to cook stuffing another 3 hours.

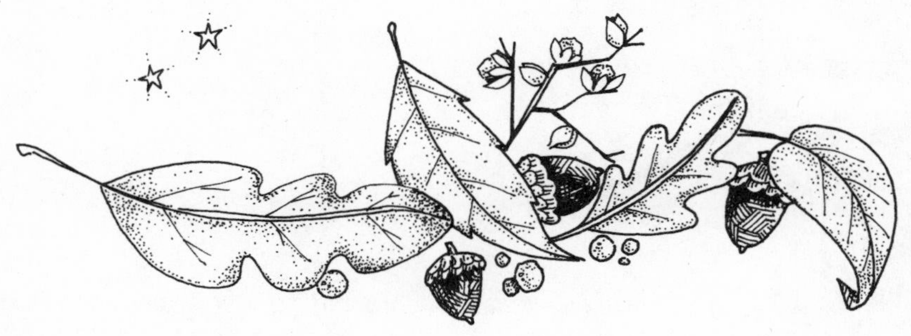

*"Come, ye thankful people, come,
Raise the song of Harvest-home."*

-Henry Alford

New England Corn Pudding

The Governor's Inn
Ludlow, VT

A wonderful, old-fashioned recipe. Make two...one is just never enough!

8 T. flour
1 t. salt
8 T. sugar
4 T. sweet, unsalted butter, melted
2 c. whole kernel corn, drained
4 lg. eggs
1 qt. whole milk

Stir the flour, salt, sugar and melted butter into the corn. Beat the eggs slightly and combine with the milk. Combine the milk and corn mixtures and pour into a 2-quart baking dish that has been sprayed with non-stick vegetable spray. Bake in a 450 degree oven for 45 minutes, until nicely browned. It's important to stir with a long-pronged fork 3 times during baking, breaking the surface as little as possible.

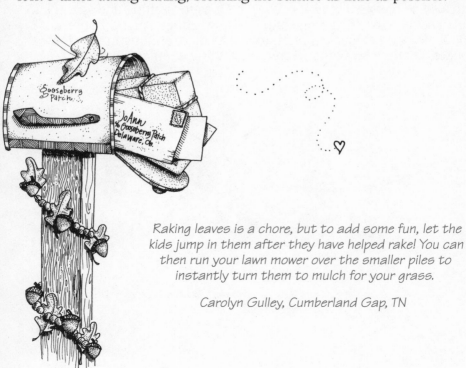

Raking leaves is a chore, but to add some fun, let the kids jump in them after they have helped rake! You can then run your lawn mower over the smaller piles to instantly turn them to mulch for your grass.

Carolyn Gulley, Cumberland Gap, TN

Old Salem Succotash

Vickie

Let this bake while you catch up with family and friends.

6 slices bacon
2 T. butter
1 sm. onion, diced
2 c. milk
1 T. brown sugar
5 c. corn kernels
4 c. lima beans
salt and pepper to taste

In a large saucepan, sauté bacon over medium heat until bacon is cooked, but not crisp. Remove bacon and set aside to cool slightly; cut into 1/2-inch pieces. Add butter and onion to saucepan and sauté for 5 minutes. Add half the bacon, milk and brown sugar, bring to a simmer. Add corn and beans, stirring well. Sprinkle remaining bacon over top, loosely cover saucepan with foil and place in a 350 degree oven. Bake for one hour, or until beans are tender. Serves 12.

Take lots of pictures of your family gathered together at Thanksgiving. Place them in an album along with traditional Thanksgiving recipes... a wonderful collection of family memories.

Autumn Apple Salad

Linda Webb
Delaware, OH

Use different types of apples to change the taste.

2 T. sugar
2 T. green onions, sliced
1/2 t. orange zest
1/3 c. canola oil
1/4 c. orange juice
3 T. lemon juice
1 Golden Delicious apple, cored and cut into small wedges
1 Red Delicious apple, cored and cut into small wedges
leaf lettuce

Prepare dressing by combining sugar, green onions, orange zest, oil, orange juice and lemon juice in a jar with a tight-fitting lid; shake well. In a mixing bowl, combine apple wedges, toss with 2 tablespoons of dressing. Arrange leaf lettuce on serving plates, top with apple slices. Serve remaining dressing on the side. Serves 4.

Use your garden's autumn bounty to create a beautiful still life. Squash, pumpkins, onions and shallots are beautiful piled in baskets and country containers. Later, use the pumpkins and squash for soup; add onions and shallots to stews and sauces for flavor!

Potato Soufflé

The Governor's Inn
Ludlow, VT

You'll be asked for seconds!

6 c. mashed potatoes
8-oz. container whipped cream cheese with chives
2 whole eggs
1/4 c. sour cream
pinch salt
4 T. sweet unsalted butter

In a medium mixing bowl, place all ingredients and mix well. Pour into prepared 1-1/2 quart soufflé dish. Bake 45 minutes at 400 degrees.

Start a new tradition this year. Visit a local produce stand to see the great bounty of the fall harvest! As your children wander happily from basket to basket of gourds, squash, apples and pumpkins, let them help you make selections. Take pictures! When you return home think of all the fun you'll have decorating your home and porch! What a great way to celebrate fall!

Valerie Boersma, Alfred, NY

Thanksgiving Relish

Wendy Lee Paffenroth
Pine Island, NY

This also makes a tasty spread on turkey sandwiches!

3 c. raw cranberries, rinsed
2 navel or sweet oranges, peeled and sectioned
1 lg. apple, cored
1 T. orange zest
3-1/2 oz. box strawberry or raspberry gelatin
1/4-oz. pkg. unflavored gelatin
1-1/2 c. sugar
1-3/4 c. boiling water

Whirl cranberries, oranges and apple in food processor for a few seconds, the put in large bowl. Add orange zest and stir, set aside. In another bowl, mix the gelatins, sugar and water. Mix until sugar and gelatins are completely dissolved. Stir into the cranberry mixture for 5 minutes until cool and evenly mixed. Pour into a mold or a bowl for Thanksgiving, or spoon into pint jars. Refrigerate at least 2 days before using, to allow flavors to blend. Makes 4 to 6 servings.

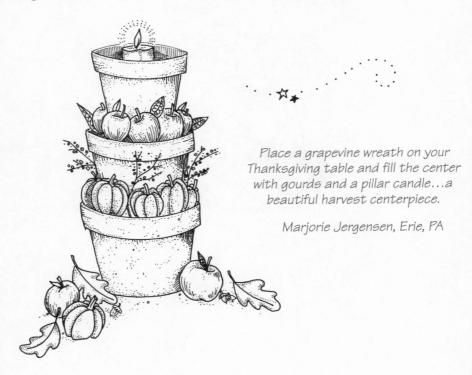

Place a grapevine wreath on your Thanksgiving table and fill the center with gourds and a pillar candle...a beautiful harvest centerpiece.

Marjorie Jergensen, Erie, PA

Mom's Best Rolls

Becky Smith
Maryville, MO

This recipe is over 20 years old...perfect for all family get-togethers!

2 pkgs. fast-rise yeast
3 c. warm water
3 eggs, beaten
1-1/2 c. sugar
2 t. salt
1/2 c. oil
9 to 11 c. flour

Mix all ingredients together and knead until smooth and elastic. Begin by mixing in 8 to 9 cups of flour, and then kneading the rest in. Turn into a large greased pan and cover; place in a warm place to rise. Punch down when double then let rise again until double in bulk. Shape into rolls, cover and let rise until double again. Bake at 300 degrees, for 25 to 30 minutes. Makes 3 to 4 dozen rolls.

Enjoy the simple pleasures of autumn. Watch the sun go down, linger in the crisp air, bring home a pot of mums for your table, build a fire in the fireplace, light candles, make taffy apples, enjoy fresh apple cider and slip into your favorite sweater.

New England Pumpkin Pie

Joan Merling
Bethel, CT

Make this special pie for your gathering.

6 T. brown sugar
2 T. sugar
1/2 t. salt
2 t. cinnamon
1/2 t. nutmeg
1/4 t. cloves
1/2 c. molasses
3 eggs, separated
2 c. cooked pumpkin
1-1/2 c. light cream
2 T. rum
1 unbaked 10" pie shell

Combine sugars, salt and spices. Add molasses and egg yolks. Mix well. Stir in pumpkin, cream and rum. Beat egg whites until stiff; fold into pumpkin mixture. Pour filling into pie shell. Bake at 425 degrees for 45 minutes, or until knife inserted in center comes out clean.

Set your Thanksgiving table festively! Use old jello molds, heart and star shapes are fun, and tuck a votive in the middle. Use cranberries or rose hips to hold the votive in place... beautiful at each place setting!

Sherian Oakley, Tullahoma, TN

Decorating
Home & Hearth

Stacey Weichert
Moorhead, MN

A harvest garland is a beautiful autumn decoration. You'll need 5 ears of large Indian corn. Holding each piece securely on a wooden board, cut the corn into 1-1/2 inch coins and drill a hole in the center of each coin. Tie a 3" loop in a 45" length of jute and thread the other end through a tapestry needle with a large eye. Begin stringing the corn and then alternating it with groups of lemon leaves (you'll need approximately 100 to complete the garland.) When you've reached the end, remove the needle and tie a loop at the end. Tie a raffia bow or ribbons on each end of the garland and stretch it across your hearth or window top. I hang mine across my windowboxes!

Katheryn Kwiatkowski
St. Paul, NE

Autumn! Just saying the word makes me feel warm! Here in Nebraska we have perfect days for curling up with a country magazine in the garden or taking walks in the country. The feel of the late summer sun and the smells of harvest are just wonderful! One of my favorite things to do is make an old-fashioned canning jar bouquet. Just take a paper sack and a pair of scissors along on one of your country walks. Gather grasses, cattails, bittersweet and goldenrod. When you get home, arrange your "harvest" in the jars. Tie a raffia bow around the jar neck for a finishing touch. A beautiful way to bring autumn indoors. You can also share them with friends and family; they'll be delighted!

A crispness in the autumn air means that the birds will soon be at your winter feeders...don't forget to stock them with seed!

Linda Stern
Columbus, OH

A Sweet Annie wreath is a beautiful and fragrant way to celebrate the autumn harvest. In the late fall, gather sprigs of the herb Sweet Annie. Easily grown in any spot of your garden that has full sun, it's a beautiful tall herb, sometimes growing to 6 feet! Gather small bunches together and secure with green floral wire. Don't cut the wire, you'll use it to continue adding to your wreath. Gently shape the wreath into a 4" or 6" circle. Before you complete your circle, overlap the end of the wreath over the beginning to cover any wires. Attach a wire loop on the back for hanging. Hang it in any room of your home and whenever the air needs freshened, just pinch a sprig to release the sweet smell. This scent will last for almost a year.

Carol Weiss
West Bend, WI

We grow our own pumpkins each year and therefore have an abundant supply. We choose 5 or 6 medium-sized pumpkins and carve their faces, we also cut a round opening in the bottom. We pound an iron fence post into the ground, an old long shovel or broom handle also works well, and stack the pumpkins on top of one another onto the fence post. We then have an instant harvest pumpkin totem pole! Small tea lights can then be placed inside each carved pumpkin. If you are ambitious, several more pumpkins may also be carved and placed on the ground surrounding the totem pole.

Juanita Williams
Jacksonville, OR

If you're in charge of refreshments for a children's Halloween party, make a batch of Ghoul-Ade. Dissolve one envelope of unsweetened grape soft drink mix, one envelope orange-flavored mix and 2 cups sugar in 3 quarts of ice water in a non-metal pitcher. Add one liter of chilled ginger ale, or use a liter of root beer for a nice murky color! Orange juice made fizzy with seltzer also tastes great!

Children can make simple Halloween ghost craft by using an 8"x10" piece of plain white paper. Fill the center of the paper with a handful of peanuts. Fold up the corners and cinch the paper around the peanuts using string. After the rope has been tied, these will look like little ghosts. The kids can now color on a face for their ghost. After play, they can eat the peanuts for a snack.

Ann Fehr
Trappe, PA

An easy way to help guests find your harvest party! Gather together several terra cotta pots and plant them with colorful mums. Using waterproof paint, put your house numbers, one per pot, on the side of each pot! Line them up on the porch steps, on your sidewalk or in a windowbox. A clever way to help guests find your home!

Decorating Home & Hearth

Allison Cooper-Schreiber
Ypsilanti, MI

When the leaves' colors are at their prime, and before they have started to fall, select large branches with a variety of colors. Take each branch and cut the stems at a sharp angle. Split the stems by cutting a slit 2 or 3 inches up the stem. Using a wooden board, crush the lower part of the stem with a hammer or mallet. Place the branches in a large, deep container filled with warm water for 2 to 3 hours.

In a large saucepan on the stove, prepare a solution of 2 parts hot water to one part glycerine, which your local pharmacy should carry. Let the mixture come to a rolling boil, then reduce the temperature to a simmer for 10 to 12 minutes. Let the mixture completely cool. Remove the branches from the warm water and fill the container with the water and glycerine mixture. Stand the prepared branches in the glycerine mixture and store in a cool, dry location until the glycerine has been completely absorbed; usually within 7 to 10 days. When tiny beads of glycerine form on the leaves, remove the stems from the container and wipe dry. The leaves will now be preserved, keeping their beautiful colors intact so you can enjoy their beauty for several years. My favorite place to put the preserved leaves is on the fireplace mantel or the dining room table surrounded by gourds, small pumpkins, vines and other seasonal decorations.

On a sunny, fall day when the leaves are turning, take your kids on a nature walk through the woods. Pick up brightly colored leaves, acorns, walnuts and bitter-sweet. When you return home, add mini Indian corn and make a fall garland, or just toss everything in a wooden bowl for homemade harvest potpourri!

Stephanie L. McAtee, Kansas City, MO

Juanita Williams
Jacksonville, OR

Easy table decorations for an autumn party can be made from milk bottles. Plan ahead for your event by purchasing milk in glass bottles in the one-quart size, saving the glass bottle for the vase. If you can't find glass milk bottles in your area, perhaps you can check with a local dairy, they have been known to sell old bottles. Purchase bolts of 6" wide ribbon in autumn colors such as gold, barn red, navy, rust, or green, at your local craft store. For each bottle you will need to combine 2 colors and will use approximately one yard of each color per bottle. Simply combine both lengths of ribbon and tie a large bow around the neck of the milk bottle. Puff up the bow and let the ends stream down almost to the end of the bottle; trim the ends evenly. These bottles can be made up quite easily ahead of time; fill with water and just tuck in a sunflower, several mums, or zinnias before your guests arrive.

Jeannine English
Wylie, TX

To create a quick and elegant look for the harvest season, fill a galvanized bucket with apples, pumpkins, or gourds. Purchase very long taper candles and insert them down in the bucket using the apples, pumpkins and gourds to anchor them. On cool, still nights, light the candles; they look especially festive on a porch!

To preserve autumn blooms, pick flowers after the dew has dried. Strip stems off leaves and hang them in a cool, dark place with good air circulation.

Janet Thomas
Mesquite, TX

I love to throw last year's pumpkin seeds in my garden. The next season, around late August or September, mini pumpkins are everywhere! I harvest my little patch and put them in a basket, giving them to each guest who enters. I also let the little ones in the neighborhood choose their own, right off the vine!

Ronda Lawson
Pleasanton, CA

Take one medium, well-rounded pumpkin. Cut off the top and thoroughly clean out the inside. If desired, use paint or a marker to create a Jack-o'-Lantern face on the outside. Set a plastic bowl inside the pumpkin and fill it with spiced cider or your favorite holiday drink. Use a punch bowl ladle to serve!

Jana Warnell
Kalispell, MT

One of my favorite Halloween gifts to make are candy corn pots. Use a terra cotta pot of any size, paint the outside white. Divide pot into thirds and paint the middle third orange. Paint the bottom third yellow and top third white. I have found that each color needs 2 coats of paint. For a nose, buy a small wooden button or knob, found at any craft store, and paint it yellow. When the button is dry, glue it to the pot. For cheeks, mix some orange and white together and dab on beside nose. Add a crooked mouth and eyes with a permanent black market and fill with candy corn!

Jeannine English
Wylie, TX

Make a unique harvest chandelier out of an old branch, some wire and small terra cotta pots filled with votive candles! Place a piece of aluminum foil in the bottom of each clay pot to cover the drainage hole, then wire as many clay pots as you'd like to a tree branch. Begin by making a wire loop the size of the clay pot. Slip it over the bottom of the pot and slide it up until it's tightly under the clay pot lip, adjusting the size if needed. Continue with your remaining clay pots making sure you wire each securely to the branch.Tuck a votive in each terra cotta pot and then suspend your branch chandelier from hooks in the ceiling...a beautiful, rustic addition to your porch or cabin!

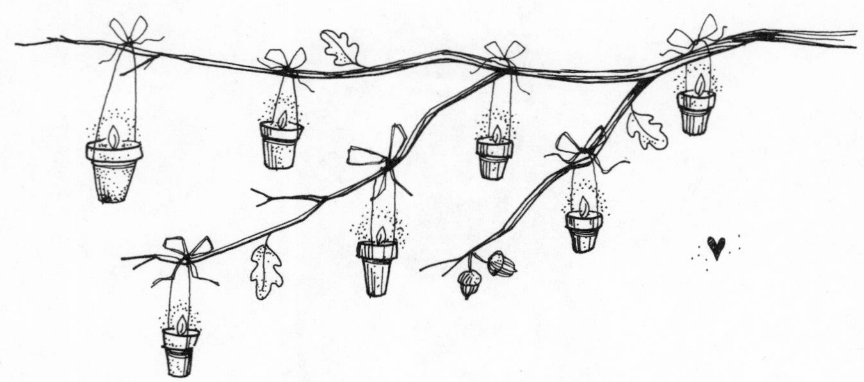

Yarrow dries very well and looks pretty displayed in baskets or in a blue pitcher for a French country look.

Kristine Gilbert
Bath, NY

I take a large grapevine wreath and tie assorted small gourds, small colorful Indian corn and a few cookie cutters to it with natural raffia and then make a large raffia bow. This wreath easily keeps from mid-September through Thanksgiving and looks wonderful inside or on the front door. You can also use cinnamon sticks, fall leaves, acorns...it's quick, easy and beautiful.

For my table, I use baby bear pumpkins, and assorted gourds as candle holders. Take your chosen gourd and make sure it can stand on its own. At the top, trace around a tealight and then carve out so that the tealight will fit in nicely.

Tina Ledbetter
Moreno Valley, CA

I like to use place cards to spruce up my table. Purchase enough 1-1/2" small terra cotta pots to put next to each place setting. Put a small bunch of wheat stalks in the center and tie the wheat with a raffia bow. Fill the pot with Spanish moss and add a place card in the center of the pot.

A cup of mulled cider is a special treat if you've been raking leaves all afternoon!

Patricia Kapusta
Bethel Park, PA

I hang fresh grapevines across the top and sides of my porch for the harvest season. You can also attach preserved fall leaves and tiny white lights to your grapevine. I gather several corn stalk bundles and place on each side of the porch as well as around the trunk of a big tree in my front yard. I then place pumpkins, gourds, mums and other harvest items by the corn stalks. It's a terrific display that lasts the whole harvest season...September through Thanksgiving!

Denise Rounds
Tulsa, OK

When we began to host Thanksgiving at our house, we started new traditions that we still do 10 years later. When I begin shopping for our meal, we select apples, oranges, persimmons, squash, carrots and nuts for our table centerpiece. We take a walk in the cool air and gather colorful fallen leaves and clip berries from our shrubs to add to the table too. We then buy a medium pumpkin and hot glue Spanish moss, pine cones, nuts, berries and leaves on the top surrounding the stem. This serves as the very center of our table. We then lay the fruit, vegetables, leaves, nuts and berries we've gathered around the base of the pumpkins. It makes a lovely natural centerpiece that the kids take pride in. As I cook, the kids prepare personal place cards for each guest using stickers and drawings. They help me set the table and decide who will sit where. These little touches have given my children a sense of fun and thankfulness.

Make your scarecrow more weather-resistant by stuffing him with crumpled newspaper you've put into plastic bags!

Priscilla Hopkins
Broomfield, CO

Here is a quick and easy harvest craft; I've even made them in my Sunday school class with the kids and the moms always rave! Using a Jack-be-Little pumpkin, cut off the top and scoop out the seeds, carving the opening just large enough for a taper candle to fit into. Insert a taper candle…yellow, brown, orange or even black for Halloween. Using a glue gun, attach some Spanish moss around the candle's base. These look wonderful anywhere in your home and great on the Thanksgiving table!

Trish Miller
Baltimore, MD

In the fall season I like to decorate with an array of gourds, Indian corn, hay and leaves in my windowboxes. As the leaves come off the trees, I also enjoy making a leaf garland. Thread the leaves on fishing line, thread, or jute just as you would string popcorn. The nice thing about the leaf garland is you don't have to use a needle to thread them, so children can have fun helping you with this craft. I glue acorns on the ends of the garland to add an extra fall touch. You can also hang this around your mantel or doorway.

Anne Frampton
Sykesville, MD

Without even carving a pumpkin, you can use one to decorate your porch or steps from September through Thanksgiving. You'll need one pumpkin, 3 ears of Indian corn, one yard of 2" paper ribbon and 2, 12" pieces of fine gauge wire. Smooth out husks on corn. If needed, the husks can be dampened, smoothed out and left to dry overnight. A husk can be coaxed into a corkscrew curl by dampening, curling around your forefinger and anchoring with a straight pin. Let dry overnight.

Using one piece of wire, wire the ears of corn together where the cobs meet the husks. Leave 2 fairly long tails of wire. Decide which is the front of your pumpkin. As you look at the front of your pumpkin, use the wire tails to attach the bunch of corn to the pumpkin stalk. Wrap the wires around the stalk a few times and twist in the back to finish off. I like to attach the corn so it is sloping at an angle across the pumpkin. Make a beautiful bow out of the ribbon and wire to the front of the pumpkin stalk so that it covers the junctions where the corn is wired to the pumpkin.

It's easy to quickly make several small pumpkins to give as treats to neighbors, co-workers, or leave on the porch of your secret pal. They make great centerpieces and can be placed on banquet tables for church or club dinners. Larger pumpkins look pretty as decorations for the hearth, front porch, foyer, or front steps. When the pumpkin finally begins to soften, cut it open and put it and the Indian corn outside as a winter treat for the outside critters.

Bake a batch of old-fashioned sugar cookies. Use a cookie stamp to press a pumpkin, leaf or apple design on top...a wonderful after-school treat for the kids!

Decorating Home & Hearth

Susan Brzozowski
Ellicott City, MD

You can make beautiful fall napkin holders from autumn treasures that are right at your feet! You'll need an 8" piece of 19 gauge wire, hot glue gun, nuts and colorful leaves collected from your yard. Wrap wire around an empty container that once held a roll of film. This will give you a uniform diameter for each holder. Twist the ends together securing a few leaves. Add a few nuts with glue. This hides the wire ends, too. Slip a pretty napkin through the loop of wire. This makes a lovely addition to your table and can even be used as a favor for your guests.

Robin Gilmore
Millbrae, CA

My favorite thing to do for our Thanksgiving gathering is to collect a variety of large fallen leaves and use them for place cards and the centerpiece on the table. I write each guest's name on a leaf with a metallic gold pen and then place the leaf on top of the napkin next to their place setting. I then spread more leaves around simple pillar candles for the centerpiece. My children love to walk and collect the leaves with me and my guests love the autumn feel of the table.

At autumn harvest, wrap any remaining green tomatoes in newspaper and store in a warm spot; they'll slowly ripen for you to enjoy later!

Heather Alexander
Lacey, WA

For fun pumpkin toppers, you'll need scrap fabric, silk flowers, silk autumn leaves, small artificial fruit picks, a hot glue gun and pinking shears. Cut a 6" circle out of your fabric, then cut a 2" circle out of the center of the first circle. Glue assorted fall leaves around the fabric, slightly overlapping. Glue the silk flowers and fruit in an attractive arrangement on top of the leaves. Place your pumpkin topper over the stem of a pumpkin. Beautiful! These can be made in a variety of sizes to make an attractive arrangement with many different sized pumpkins.

Lori Triplett
Westminster, MD

Using the Williamsburg-style welcome plaque for inspiration, you can have a beautiful harvest welcome for over your entrance door! If you make this in September, it will last through Thanksgiving until you make another one for the Christmas season. Cut a semi-circular wood base to fit over your door. Cover it with corn stalks, pulling back the husks to let the corn show. Attach a pumpkin to the center and, using nails or a glue gun, add gourds, Indian corn, nuts and preserved fall leaves, acorns and canella berries.

Denise Blaine
Sheppard Air Force Base, TX

Fabric pumpkins are quick to make and wonderful decorations from September to Thanksgiving. Place together 2 pieces of 10"x12" orange fabric, rights sides facing. Cut along one of the 10" sides with pinking sheers, this will be the top of your pumpkin. Sew the remaining 12" sides together with a straight-stitch. Loosely whip-stitch the remaining 10" side, this will be the bottom of your pumpkin. After you've loosely stitched the bottom, tightly pull on the thread. This will create a slightly gathered bottom for your pumpkin. Turn the fabric right side out and stuff with fiberfill to within 2" of the top. Gather the top together, tucking a short twig inside for your pumpkin stem. Tie with jute. You can even add a piece of green fabric tied in a tight knot around the twig for your pumpkin leaves. So easy and will take less than 10 minutes to make!

Marion Pfeifer
Smyrna, DE

Make a Halloween birdhouse! Paint the front of the birdhouse orange and the sides and back black. Stencil an orange and black checkerboard on the roof. On the front of your birdhouse, paint black or yellow eyes and a mouth, leaving the bird entrance for your Jack-o'-Lantern's nose!

Dress up to greet your
trick-or-treaters!

Gina Harrell
Savannah, GA

I live in the South where the weather stays warm long into the harvest season, so I can't burn a fire in the fireplace until almost Christmas. To create a nice cozy glow, I put large candles of various heights in the fireplace. I then add a few harvest picks, such as nuts, pumpkins, or greenery. The fireplace looks beautiful lit up and it doesn't heat the house!

Eleanor Makulinski
Sylvania, OH

Since we have a large family, we always have meals buffet-style. I like to make the table festive, so I always make a pretty centerpiece for the middle of our large table. I purchase a pumpkin and use it as a container for my wildflowers and mums. Just remove the top and scoop out the seeds and pulp. We also surround the pumpkin with pinecones, acorns and evergreen boughs. It makes such a nice centerpiece at Thanksgiving.

Darlene Marchina
Crown Point, IN

On Halloween, after trick-or-treating, I always invite my nieces and a few neighborhood friends of my sons for a little pumpkin party. We play a game of Pin the Nose on the Pumpkin! I make a pumpkin from orange construction paper, add eyes and a mouth and leave a big empty space for the nose. We cut triangular noses from construction paper, add a loop of tape to the back and have the blindfolded children try to place the nose in the right spot! We then decorate cupcakes with sprinkles, candy corn, jelly beans and licorice. It's a great way to wind down the evening.

Beginning in October, water your rhododendrons thoroughly every two weeks until the ground freezes.

The Christmas Pantry

Banana Orange Bread

Ruth Palmer
Glendale, UT

Salt and sugar-free...but still delicious!

2 c. flour
1 t. baking powder
1 t. soda
1 t. pumpkin pie spice
6-oz. can orange juice concentrate
2 ripe bananas
2 eggs
1 c. raisins
1 c. walnuts

Mix dry ingredients together. Blend orange juice, bananas and eggs together. Stir in raisins and nuts. Pour mixture into a 9"x4" greased loaf pan and bake at 350 degrees for 35 minutes. Cool on a rack before cutting into 9 one-inch slices. May be served hot or cold, plain or with cream cheese and butter.

"I will honor Christmas in my heart, and try to keep it all the year."

-Charles Dickens

Cinnamon-Cocoa Rolls

Carol Bull
Gooseberry Patch

Wake your family up to the aroma of freshly baked rolls!

1-1/4 c. skim milk
1 pkg. dry yeast
2 T. sugar
1/4 c. stick margarine, melted
1/2 t. vanilla extract
1 egg, lightly beaten
4 c. bread flour, divided
1/3 c. unsweetened cocoa
1/2 t. salt
1 egg white, lightly beaten
1/4 c. sugar
1 t. ground cinnamon
1 c. powdered sugar, sifted
2 T. skim milk
1 t. vanilla extract

Warm milk to 105-115 degrees. Dissolve yeast and 2 tablespoons sugar in milk in a large bowl; let stand 5 minutes. Add margarine, vanilla and egg; stir well. Stir in 3-1/2 cups flour, cocoa and salt to form a soft dough. Turn dough out onto a lightly floured surface and knead until smooth and elastic, about 10 minutes; add enough of the remaining flour, one tablespoon at a time, to prevent dough from sticking to hands. Place dough in a large bowl coated with cooking spray, turning to coat top. Cover and let rise in a warm place free from drafts, 45 minutes or until doubled in bulk. Punch dough down. Turn out onto a lightly floured surface; roll into a 16"x8" rectangle. Brush egg white over entire surface. Combine sugar and cinnamon; sprinkle evenly over dough. Starting at long side, roll up dough tightly, jelly-roll fashion; pinch seam to seal, do not seal ends of roll. Cut roll into 16 one-inch slices, using string or dental floss. Arrange slices, cut sides up, in a 19"x13" baking pan coated with cooking spray. Cover and let rise 30 minutes or until doubled in bulk. Preheat oven to 350 degrees; bake rolls at 350 degrees for 20 minutes. Combine remaining ingredients; stir well. Drizzle over rolls. Makes 16 servings.

Mom's Applesauce Bread

Emily Johnson
Pocatello, ID

Fill your kitchen with the aroma of apple and spices from this good and simple recipe.

1/2 c. butter
1 c. sugar
1 egg
1 t. cinnamon
1/2 t. cloves
1 c. applesauce
1 t. baking soda
1/4 t. salt
2 c. flour
1 c. raisins

Mix ingredients together. Bake in a loaf pan at 350 degrees for 45 to 60 minutes.

Spiced Honey

Kathy Grashoff
Ft. Wayne, IN

Good on toast, scones, biscuits or homemade bread!

5 whole cloves
5 whole allspice berries
1 pt. honey
1/4 t. nutmeg, grated
2 cinnamon sticks

Place cloves and allspice berries in a pint jar. Pour honey over spices and stir in nutmeg. Add cinnamon sticks and loosely cover jar with plastic wrap. Place the jar in a container of warm water and allow to stand until the water has cooled. Remove jar from water and place metal lid on securely. Let honey sit one week to allow flavors to blend. Makes 2 cups.

"There seems a magic the very name of Christmas!"

-Charles DIckens

Cinnamon Puffins

Emily Jordan
Delaware, OH

Wonderful on a cold winter's morn!

1-1/2 c. flour
1-1/2 t. baking powder
1/2 t. salt
1 t. nutmeg, ground and divided
1/3 c. shortening
1 c. sugar, divided
1 egg
1/2 t. vanilla extract
1/2 c. milk
1/2 c. butter
1 t. cinnamon, ground

Preheat oven to 350 degrees. In medium mixing bowl, combine flour, baking powder, salt and 1/2 teaspoon nutmeg. In another bowl, beat shortening, 1/2 cup sugar, egg and vanilla until well blended. Add the flour mixture to the creamed mixture and beat in the milk until smooth. Fill each greased cup 2/3 full with batter. Bake 20 minutes. Melt butter in small pan. In small bowl, combine 1/2 cup sugar, cinnamon and 1/2 teaspoon nutmeg. While puffins are warm, dip each one in butter, then in sugar mixture. Store in an airtight container.

Tie colorful ribbon on all your throw pillows to make them look like packages! You can use wide satin ribbon, plaid, or velvet...it looks as if there are packages everywhere!

Linda Thompson, Mt. Juliet, TN

German Kuchen

Pat Buckel
Erie, PA

Make this German coffee cake a tradition in your family.

2 pkgs. dry yeast
2-1/2 c. water, lukewarm
7-1/2 c. flour
1/2 t. baking powder
1/2 t. baking soda
1 T. salt
1 c. sugar
1 egg
1/2 c. margarine, melted
sugar and cinnamon

Dissolve yeast in 1/2 cup water, add remaining 2 cups water. Sift and measure 4 cups flour with baking powder, baking soda, salt and sugar. Add to yeast mixture. Add egg and beat. Add margarine and beat. Add remaining flour. Mix and knead. Let rise until double in size. Shape and let rise until double in slightly greased pans. Sprinkle mixture of sugar and cinnamon on top of each before second rise. Bake at 400 degrees for 10 to 15 minutes. Makes 4 round kuchens.

Prop an old sled on your front porch and hang a wreath or a pair of old ice skates on it! Add a little bit of evergreen and grapevine... it's a wonderfully nostalgic welcome.

Missy Volkmann, Sauk Centre, MN

Honey French Toast

Karla Nitz
Janesville, WI

A no-fuss recipe!

3 eggs
3/4 c. milk
1/2 t. vanilla
1 T. honey
8 slices bread, slightly dry
1 c. cereal, crushed

Mix together the eggs, milk, vanilla and honey. Dip both sides of bread into the mixture and then into the crushed cereal mixture. Place bread onto greased cookie sheets and bake at 350 degrees for 7 to 9 minutes. At this point, the French toast can be served with butter and syrup or frozen and later warmed up in microwave or toaster.

Fill a variety of glass jars with colorful Christmas candies, one kind per jar. Gumdrops, candy canes, red licorice and hard candies look tasty! Tie a red or gold bow around each jar and group them on a table or countertop.

Kathleen Schuller, Sylvania, OH

Breakfast Potato Pie

Rachel Keller
Provo, UT

Known as Pastel de Papas in Argentina, this is terrific for breakfast or brunch.

4 large potatoes, cubed
double crust pie crust, unbaked
1 c. Cheddar cheese, cubed
1 c. ham, cubed
5 eggs
salt and pepper to taste

Cover potatoes with water and boil until tender, approximately 20 minutes. Fill pie crust with potatoes. Sprinkle with Cheddar cheese and ham. Beat eggs together in small bowl and season with salt and pepper. Pour eggs over pie and cover pie with top crust. Bake at 350 degrees for 45 minutes.

Use small jelly jars as candle holders! Fill the jars half full with rock salt and tuck a tea light or votive in the salt, tie a raffia ribbon around the bottom of the jars.

Phyllis Stout
East Palatka, FL

Puffed Apple Pancakes

Cheryl Flynn
Mt. Sterling, IL

You can use egg substitutes in this recipe if you prefer.

6 large eggs
1-1/2 c. milk
1 c. flour
1/3 c. sugar
2 t. vanilla
1/2 t. salt
2 t. cinnamon
1 stick butter
2 apples, peeled & thinly sliced
brown sugar

Preheat oven to 425 degrees. In a blender or large bowl, mix eggs, milk, flour, sugar, vanilla, salt and cinnamon, until well blended. Place butter in a 13"x9" pan, put in oven and allow to melt; do not brown. Remove pan from oven, add apple slices and pour egg mixture over apples. Sprinkle with brown sugar to taste. Bake at 425 degrees for 20 minutes or until puffy and brown. Serves 6 to 8.

Place a pillar candle on a holiday plate, place the hurricane globe over the candle, then fill the globe three-quarters full with fresh cranberries...be sure to let most of the candle appear above the cranberries. Arrange fresh greens around the base of the candle for a terrific centerpiece!

Judi Mohr, Plymouth, MN

Cranberry Coffee Cake

Pat DePond
St. Charles, MO

Serve this in a tube pan for family breakfast, or in loaf pans for gifts!

1/2 c. butter
1 c. sugar
2 eggs
1 t. baking soda
1 t. baking powder
2 c. flour
1/2 t. salt
8-oz. carton sour cream
1 t. almond extract
7-oz. can whole cranberries, drained
1/2 c. pecans, chopped

Cream butter and sugar together. Add eggs, one at a time, mixing well after each addition. In a large bowl, combine next 4 dry ingredients well and add to egg mixture alternately with sour cream. Blend in almond extract. Lightly oil and flour a tube pan, or two 9"x5" loaf pans. Layer coffee cake mixture and cranberries, ending with coffee cake mixture. Sprinkle pecans over top. Bake at 350 degrees for 55 minutes, cool completely. Drizzle with topping.

Topping:

3/4 c. powdered sugar
2 T. water
1/2 t. almond extract

Combine ingredients, blending well. Drizzle over cooled coffee cake.

Damascus Brick Sweet Rolls

The Damascus Brick
Junction City, OH

There's nothing like the smell of fresh breads baking to welcome guests. The memories and smells of their childhood soon warm their hearts.

1 c. milk
1/2 c. butter
2 t. salt
1/2 c. plus 1 t. sugar, divided
2 T. yeast
1 c. warm water
1 egg, beaten
6 to 7 cups bread flour
cinnamon
sugar
1 stick butter

Combine milk, butter, salt and 1/2 cup sugar in a saucepan until just warm. In a small mixing bowl, combine yeast and water until yeast is dissolved; add remaining sugar. When yeast mixture begins to foam, add to milk mixture; mix well. Fold in egg. Add flour and blend thoroughly. Roll dough out on a floured surface, sprinkle with cinnamon and sugar to taste, dot with butter as desired. Roll dough lengthwise and cut into one-inch slices. Place on a lightly oiled cookie sheet and let rise until double. Bake at 375 degrees for 12 to 15 minutes. Ice if desired. Makes 2 dozen rolls.

Make a batch of old-fashioned fudge!

Praline Apple Bread

Becky Sykes
Gooseberry Patch

This is so good!

1 c. sugar
8 oz. sour cream
2 eggs
2 t. vanilla
2 c. all-purpose flour
2 t. baking powder
1/2 t. baking soda
1/2 t. salt
1-1/4 c. tart apples, peeled and chopped
1 c. pecans, chopped

In a large mixing bowl, beat together sugar, sour cream, eggs and vanilla on low speed until combined. Beat on medium speed 2 minutes. Stir together flour, baking powder, soda and salt; add to sour cream mixture, beating on low until thoroughly mixed. Stir in apple and 1/2 cup pecans. Turn into a greased 9"x5"x3" loaf pan. Sprinkle with remaining pecans; press lightly into batter. Bake at 350 degrees for 55 to 60 minutes, or until a toothpick inserted in the center comes out clean. Cool in pan on a wire rack for 10 minutes. While bread is cooling, prepare icing.

Icing:

1/4 c. butter
1/4 c. brown sugar, packed

In a small saucepan combine butter and brown sugar; cook and stir until mixture comes to a boil. Reduce heat and boil gently for one minute. Remove bread from pan. Drizzle with brown sugar mixture; cool. Serves 18.

Make snow ice cream! A wonderful winter treat!

Christmas Cranberry Muffins

Beth Warner
Delaware, OH

Creates a wonderful aroma while baking; and so colorful, too!

2 c. flour
1 c. sugar
1-1/2 t. baking powder
1/2 t. baking soda
1/2 t. salt
2 T. shortening
1 orange, juiced and grated
water
1 egg, beaten
1 c. raw cranberries, halved

Preheat oven to 350 degrees. In a large bowl combine first 5 ingredients, blend in shortening. Add orange rind. Place juice from orange in a 3/4 cup measure and add enough water to bring liquid equal to 3/4 cup. Blend into flour mixture. Add egg and fold in cranberries. Pour into greased muffin cups, filling 2/3 full. Bake at 350 degrees for 15 to 18 minutes, remove from pan and cool on a rack. Makes approximately 18 muffins. This can also be made into quick bread by pouring batter into an oiled bread pan and baking at 350 degrees for 50 to 60 minutes.

Decorate your bay window to look like a toy store window! Bring out a variety of stuffed animals, wrapped packages, festive decorations, a train set, dolls or even a tiny decorated tree!

Balynda Elkins, Paulding, OH

Grandma's Pancakes

Joni Smyth
Delaware, OH

These are light & fluffy!

4 eggs, separated
2 c. flour
3 t. baking powder
1 t. salt
2 c. milk

Beat egg whites together until stiff peaks form; set aside. In a large bowl, blend remaining ingredients, including egg yolks. Fold in egg whites. Lightly oil skillet and spoon in 1/4 cup of pancake batter for each pancake. When bubbles form on top, turn pancake. Continue to cook until golden on bottom.

Make stars from twigs in your own backyard! Tie them together with jute then hang them from the ceiling for a "starry night" effect!

Penny McShane, Lombard, IL

Sunset Orchard Spiced Tea Mix

Leekay Bennett
Gooseberry Patch

Warm & spicy! Enjoy this Christmas morning!

1 c. sugar
1/3 c. dry orange drink mix
2/3 c. dry instant tea
2 envelopes (.65 or .72 oz. each) instant spiced cider mix

Combine sugar, drink mix and tea together. Blend in cider mix. Place in an airtight container. For each 7 ounces of hot water used, add 3-1/2 teaspoons of mix; let steep 2 minutes.

On Christmas Eve, a short time before bedtime, have the kids get in their jammies, pack a couple of quilts and jump into the family car and "tour" the neighborhood looking at all the Christmas lights! Keep the heater low so it's a little chilly in the car...everyone can snuggle under the quilts and enjoy the lights! At our house Grandma loves this tradition. She says it's such a treat to cuddle with her grandsons and also to be chauffeured around!

Susan Kennedy, Gooseberry Patch

Reuben Spread

Peggy Jasenski
Greenville, OH

Serve this on mini rye bread...wonderful!

3 pkgs. dried beef, chopped
16-oz. can sauerkraut, drained
1/2 lb. Swiss cheese, shredded
1/2 lb. Cheddar cheese, shredded
1 c. mayonnaise

Combine all ingredients and bake in a lightly oiled casserole dish at 350 degrees for 25 to 30 minutes.

If you have young toddlers who can't sign their names yet, have them place their hands on a stamp pad and then press their hands on your holiday cards! Relatives love to see how the kids have grown!

Angela Harmon, Bartlett, TN

Cheesy Bread

Tammy McCartney
Oxford, OH

Wonderful with soup on a cold, snowy, winter day.

1 loaf bakery French bread
8-oz. pkg. sliced Swiss cheese
2 T. onion, chopped
1 T. dry mustard
1 T. poppy seeds
1 t. seasoned salt
2 sticks margarine, melted

Using a serrated bread knife, cut diagonal slits in the bread, going almost all the way through. Put the bread on a large piece of foil, then on a cookie sheet. In the slits place pieces of the Swiss cheese. Combine the last 5 ingredients and pour over the bread. Wrap the foil around the bread. Bake at 350 degrees for 35 to 40 minutes. Serve warm.

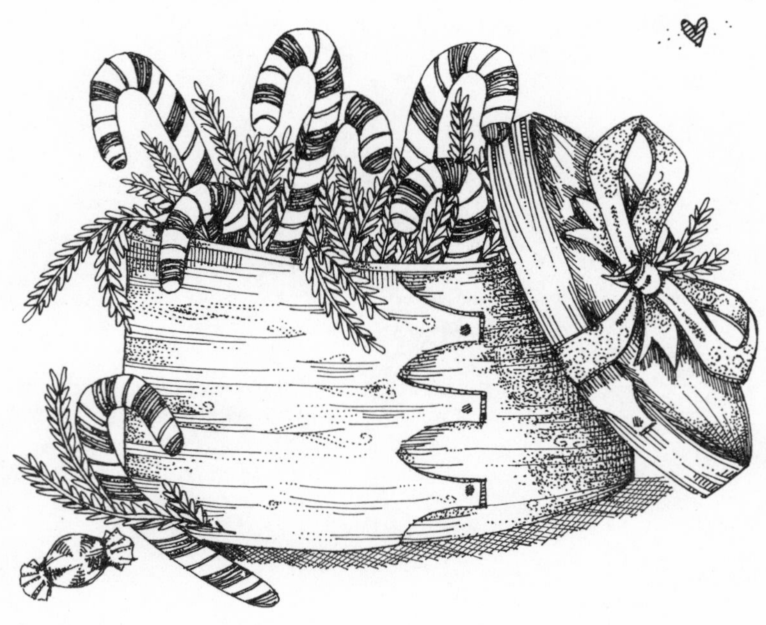

Instead of Christmas stockings, give everyone their own holiday basket. Fill each basket with stocking stuffers then hang them from hooks on the mantel.

Michelle Urdahl, Litchfield, MN

Grandma B's Swedish Meatballs

Eloise Bigham
Greenville, OH

Easy to make!

2 lbs. hamburger
1 c. cracker crumbs
1/2 t. salt
2 eggs, beaten
1 t. garlic, minced
1 T. olive oil
10-oz. can cream of mushroom soup
10-oz. can cream of chicken soup
milk

Combine hamburger, cracker crumbs, salt, eggs and garlic mix well. Shape into quarter-size balls. Brown meatballs in olive oil, turning to brown thoroughly. Place meatballs in a casserole dish. Add both cans of soup to a medium mixing bowl. Add enough milk to an empty soup can to fill it halfway, then blend milk well with soups; pour over meatballs. Cover and bake at 350 degrees until bubbly. Makes 2 to 3 dozen meatballs.

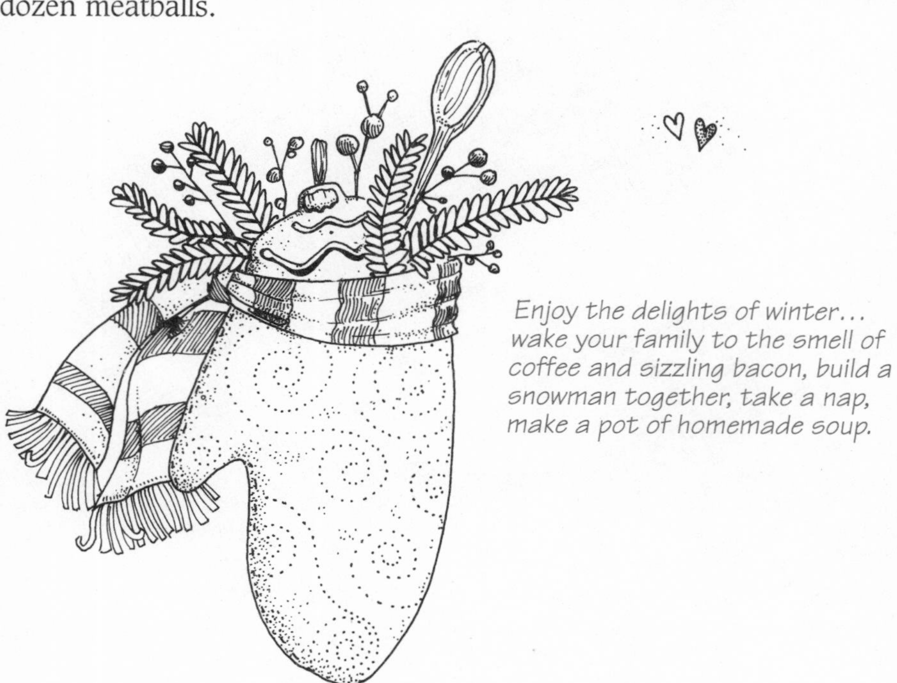

Enjoy the delights of winter... wake your family to the smell of coffee and sizzling bacon, build a snowman together, take a nap, make a pot of homemade soup.

Salmon au Gratin

Linda Gilliland
Casper, WY

This recipe was discovered in a 1918 ladies' magazine!

2 T. butter
2 T. flour
2 c. milk
14.75-oz. can of salmon, drained
1 c. bread crumbs
1 c. Cheddar cheese, grated

Make a sauce with butter, flour and milk. Boil until sauce is smooth and thick. Add salmon. Mix and pour into greased casserole or individual baking dishes. Cover top with bread crumbs and cheese. Bake at 350 degrees until brown on top. Serves 3 to 4.

Hang old-fashioned cookie cutters on red ribbons from your chandelier, then weave pine branches or garland around to create a cozy glow.

Nancy Molldrem, Eau Claire, WI

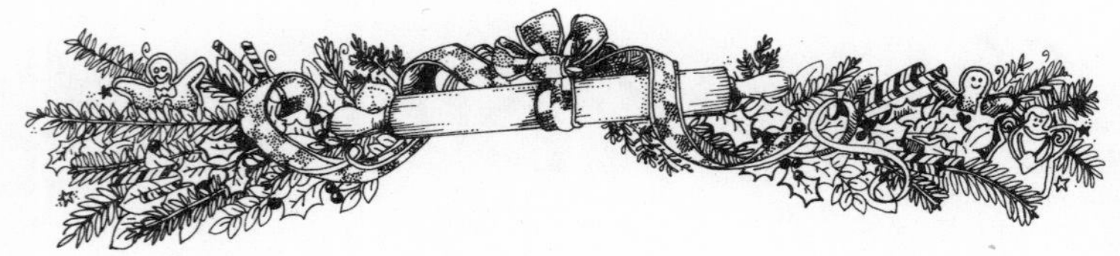

Holiday Quiche

Wendy Lee Paffenroth
Pine Island, NY

Double the recipe! Freeze the second quiche and you have a quick meal when time is short!

10-oz. pkg. frozen spinach
2 c. sharp Cheddar cheese, shredded
2 T. flour
1 c. milk
2 lg. eggs, beaten
3 slices bacon, cooked, drained and crumbled
dash black pepper
9" pie shell
Garnish: tomato wedges and fresh parsley

Cook the spinach, drain, cool and snip into small pieces. In a bowl, toss the cheese with the flour. Add the rest of the ingredients starting with the spinach and mix well. Pour into a pie shell and bake at 350 degrees for one hour. Cool slightly and slice into pieces. Garnish each slice with a wedge of tomato and parsley. Serves 6.

Fill a basket with pinecones and a short string of multi-colored mini Christmas lights. Add a pretty bow and plug in…looks beautiful!

Debbie Wakeland
Georgetown, KY

Hot Fruit Compote

Sherry Ward
Greenville, OH

You can make this a day ahead...just bake before guests arrive.

15-oz. can pear halves, cut
15-oz. can peach halves, cut
10-oz. can pineapple tidbits
11-oz. can mandarin oranges
3/4 c. brown sugar
1/2 c. margarine, melted
1-1/2 T. cornstarch
1 t. curry powder

Drain juice from all fruit. Blend fruit together and place in an 11"x7" baking dish. Combine remaining ingredients in a saucepan and heat, but not to boiling. Pour over fruit. Bake for one hour at 325 degrees.

Trace your children's or grandchildren's handprints and transfer them to light colored fabric...embroider around the handprints adding their name and the date. You can then make a small pillow, a nice gift for Mom or Grandma. You can also frame the handprint, or make them part of a special family quilt.

Mary Ann Nemecek
Springfield, IL

Amish Friendship Bread

Becky Sykes
Gooseberry Patch

Share your starter with a friend.

3 c. flour, divided
3 c. sugar, divided
3 c. milk, divided
2/3 c. oil
2 c. flour
1 c. sugar
1-1/4 t. baking powder
3 eggs
1-1/2 to 1 t. cinnamon
1 t. vanilla
1/2 t. salt
1/2 t. baking soda

Make your own starter by combining one cup flour, one cup sugar and one cup of milk in a non-metal bowl. On day one, the day you make or receive, your starter, do nothing. On days 2, 3, and 4, stir with a wooden spoon. Do not use a metal spoon. Day 5 add one cup flour, one cup sugar and one cup milk; stir. Days 6, 7, 8 and 9, stir with wooden spoon. Day 10 add one cup flour, one cup sugar and one cup milk; stir. To give the starter as gifts, pour one cup of the starter into 3 glass or plastic containers. and give to 2 friends, keeping one starter for yourself. To the remaining batch, add the remainder of the ingredients. Pour into 2 well greased and sugared loaf pans. Bake at 350 degrees for 40 to 50 minutes. Cool 10 minutes before removing from pan. Be sure to include these instructions on your gift tag when giving your starter away!

Place a greenery wreath around a plate of holiday cookies!

Kathy Grashoff, Ft. Wayne, IN

Blueberry Swirl Pound Cake

Ana Huron
Tiger, GA

Flavorful and moist!

1/2 c. shortening
1 c. butter
3 c. sugar
5 eggs
3 c. flour
1/2 t. salt
1/2 t. baking powder
1 c. milk
1 t. vanilla extract
1 t. coconut flavoring
1/2 can blueberry pie filling

Cream shortening, butter and sugar until light and fluffy. Add eggs, one at a time, beating thoroughly. Combine flour, salt and baking powder in a separate bowl. Add dry ingredients and milk, alternately, to the butter mixture, beating well after each addition. Add extracts. Mix well. Fold the blueberry filling in so as not to color the cake mix. This will give the cake a swirled look. Bake 1-1/2 hours at 325 degrees in a standard size Bundt® pan. Allow cake to cool slightly and then remove from pan. Pour glaze over cake while it is still warm. Serves 12 to 14.

Glaze:

1 c. sugar
1/4 c. water
1 t. almond extract

Cook glaze mixture until sugar is dissolved.

Invite friends over for a Christmas film-fest! Enjoy non-stop viewings of classic movies and old favorites while enjoying cocoa and dessert.

Apple Streusel Coffeecake

Patricia Shearman
Norway, ME

Perfect for apple lovers in your family!

3-1/4 c. all-purpose flour
1-1/2 t. baking powder
3/4 t. baking soda
1-1/2 sticks butter, softened
1-1/4 c. granulated sugar
3 lg. eggs
2 t. vanilla extract
16-oz. container plain low-fat yogurt
2 Granny Smith or Golden Delicious apples, peeled, cored and diced

Mix flour, baking powder and baking soda in small bowl. Beat butter and sugar in a large bowl with electric mixer until fluffy, about 2 minutes. Beat in eggs one at a time, beating well after each. Beat in vanilla and yogurt. With mixer on low speed, beat in flour mixture just until blended, scraping down bowl as necessary. Spoon 3 cups batter into a 14-cup non-stick Bundt® pan, spread evenly. Sprinkle with 1/4 cup of streusel, apples, then 1/2 cup streusel. Spoon on the remaining batter and spread evenly. Sprinkle with remaining streusel, pressing down lightly so it sticks to batter. Bake at 350 degrees for 50 to 60 minutes or until a pick comes out clean. Cool in pan on wire rack 15 minutes. Place cookie sheet over pan and carefully invert both. Remove pan and cool completely.

Streusel:

1-1/4 c. light-brown sugar
3/4 c. all-purpose flour
1 stick cold butter, cut in small pieces
2 t. cinnamon
1 c. walnuts, coarsely chopped

In a medium bowl, stir brown sugar, flour, butter and cinnamon with a fork or rub together with fingertips until crumbly and butter is completely incorporated. Stir in walnuts.

Angel Gingerbread

Karen Moran
Navasota, TX

Wonderful to have on hand during the holidays.

1 c. flour
1 t. baking soda
1/2 t. ginger
1/4 t. cinnamon
1/4 t. cloves
1/4 t. salt

1/2 c. shortening
1/2 c. sugar
1/4 c. molasses
1 egg
1/2 c. boiling water

Sift flour, measure. Sift again with soda, spices and salt. Cream shortening until soft. Beat in sugar and molasses with rotary egg beater until well blended. Add egg, beat well. Add flour mixture, blend well. Add boiling water. Stir until well blended. Bake in greased, wax paper lined 8" square pan at 350 degrees for 30 minutes. Makes 12 squares.

"Heap on more wood! The wind is chill; but let it whistle as it will, we'll keep our Christmas merry still."

-Sir Walter Scott

Fruit & Honey Dessert

Kathy Armstrong
Perrysburg, OH

Light and refreshing!

2 oranges, peeled and sectioned
1 pt. strawberries, sliced
2 apples, chopped
2 pears, sliced
2 peaches or nectarines, sliced
2 c. grapes

Add fruit together and serve with dressing.

Dressing:

2 T. honey
1/4 t. lemon peel, finely shredded
2 T. lemon juice
1-1/2 t. poppy seeds
1/4 t. dry mustard
1/3 c. salad oil

Mix together. Serve over fruit.

Brunch & Go Punch

Mary Murray
Gooseberry Patch

Perfect for the holidays!

2 qt. peppermint ice cream
1 qt. milk
1/4 t. peppermint extract
3 or 4 drops red coloring
2 qt. ginger ale

Blend 3 pints softened ice cream and milk in punch bowl. Add extract and coloring. Gradually add ginger ale, stirring gently. Cut in remaining ice cream to float in bits. Serves 32.

Paint styrofoam balls with white craft glue then roll in crushed potpourri. Pile in a bowl or basket...beautiful and easy!

Carol Young, Silver Lake, ID

Tangy Vegetable Dip

Carol Shirkey
Canton, OH

This dip won First Prize in a local recipe contest!

1 pt. mayonnaise
1/4 onion, grated
3/4 t. paprika
3/4 t. Worcestershire sauce
1/4 t. horseradish
8 to 10 drops hot pepper sauce
1/2 t. dry mustard
salt and pepper to taste

Combine all ingredients thoroughly and chill. Serve with your favorite vegetables!

Save your favorite Christmas cards and frame them. You can even then set them on an easel for tabletop decorations!

Kathleen Schuller, Sylvania, OH

Pizza Rolls

Mary Haubiel
Delaware, OH

Wonderful! These will disappear fast!

1 lb. hamburger
1 lb. sausage
2 onions, diced
3 sweet green peppers, minced
2 15-oz. cans pizza sauce
13-oz. can mushrooms, sliced
12 tubes 8-count crescent roll dough
1 pkg. pepperoni, diced
3 c. pizza cheese

Brown hamburger, sausage, onions and green peppers in a skillet. Drain excess oil. Mix in sauce and mushrooms and heat through. Separate crescent rolls and press in lightly oiled muffin pans to form a shell. Spoon in filling mixture. Top with pepperoni and cheese. Bake at 400 degrees for 10 minutes. Makes 40 to 50 rolls. You can also use mini muffin tins for tiny appetizers and any leftovers freeze well.

Cover a photo album in holiday fabric and tuck in photos of your children's past Christmases. This makes a special holiday memory book as your children grow up.

Phyllis Stout
East Palatka, FL

Tuna Puffs

Debbie Lloyd
Newark, OH

Bite-size treats!

1 c. hot water
1/2 c. butter
1 c. flour
4 eggs
1 t. onion, minced
6-1/2 oz. can tuna, drained
1/2 c. mayonnaise

Heat water and butter together in a saucepan until boiling. Remove from heat and stir in flour. Beat in eggs, one at a time. Drop on an ungreased cookie sheet and bake at 400 degrees for 30 minutes. Remove puffs from oven and let cool slightly. Combine remaining ingredients until well-blended. Split puffs and spoon tuna mixture inside.

"Chill December brings the sleet, blazing fire and Christmas treat."

-Mother Goose

Cheese Olive Dip

Carriage House Bed & Breakfast
Southaven, MI

Serve with crackers or chips.

1 c. Cheddar cheese, shredded
1 c. mayonnaise
1/2 c. onions, chopped
1/2 c. black olives, chopped

Mix thoroughly and bake in 400 degree oven for 10 minutes. Serve with crackers or chips.

Tie jingle bells to a length of jute or twine and make a festive garland for your Christmas tree!

Penny McShane
Lombard, IL

Crab Triangles

Carriage House Bed & Breakfast
Southaven, MI

A terrific warm appetizer!

1 c. crab meat, shredded
1 c. mayonnaise
1 c. mozzarella cheese, shredded
dash garlic salt
English muffin halves

Mix ingredients thoroughly and spread on English muffin halves. Cut in 4 pieces before baking. Bake at 350 degrees for 20 to 25 minutes or until light golden brown. Serve on warmer tray.

At the beginning of the holiday season, we choose a theme and host a progressive dinner with three other couples. This year the theme is Italian, next year it's Merry Olde England! After appetizers, soup and bread and finally the main course at different homes, we go caroling!

Judy Porento, Lowell, IN

Lemon Shrimp Salad

Fawn McKenzie
Butte, MT

Serve with a variety of crackers or sour dough bread.

- 8 oz. cream cheese, softened
- 10-oz. can chicken noodle soup
- 4-oz. pkg. lemon gelatin
- 1/2 c. boiling water
- 1/2 c. mayonnaise or salad dressing
- 3/4 c. celery, chopped
- 1/2 c. green onions, chopped
- 1/3 c. green peppers, chopped
- 1 small jar pimento, drained and chopped
- 6-oz. can shrimp, drained

In a medium bowl, fold cream cheese in soup until blended. In separate bowl, dissolve gelatin in boiling water and set aside to cool. Add mayonnaise to cream cheese mixture and blend. Add chopped ingredients, gelatin and shrimp. Pour into salad mold or a glass 8"x8" baking dish, and chill until set. Serves 10 to 12.

Curried Rice Salad

Wanda Rogers
Kingwood, TX

A delicious and colorful salad!

4 c. rice, cooked and chilled
4 stalks celery, diced
4 green onions with tops, finely sliced
1 med. bell pepper, diced
1/2 c. almonds, slivered
6-oz. bag fresh or frozen shrimp, thawed
10-oz. pkg. frozen green peas, thawed
11-oz. can mandarin oranges, drained
4 T. ripe olives, sliced

Mix all ingredients together and toss gently with dressing. Chill overnight.

Dressing:

1 c. mayonnaise
2 T. soy sauce
1-1/2 t. curry powder
1 t. lemon juice

Combine ingredients together.

"The whole world is a Christmas tree and stars its many candles."

-Harriet Blodgett

Cauliflower Salad

Becky Newton
Oklahoma City, OK

So quick to make.

1 lg. head of cauliflower
1 sm. can black olives, chopped or sliced
4 green onions, chopped
1/2 to 1 c. mayonnaise

Slice the cauliflower thin. Drain olives and add to cauliflower. Add chopped green onions. Add mayonnaise to lightly coat the cauliflower. Stir to chill. Serves 6 to 10.

Spell out Noel or Joy with your children's old worn out alphabet blocks. Set in a basket of evergreens or on a windowsill.

Evelyn Bruce, St. Louis, MO

Cabbage Ramen salad

Robin Kato
San Francisco, CA

Great for a crowd...doubles and triples easily!

1 lg. green cabbage, thinly sliced
1/2 med. red cabbage, thinly sliced
4 green onions, diagonally sliced
3-oz. pkg. ramen noodles, any flavor

Cut green cabbage head in quarters. Slice quarters thinly from tip to base. Remove any large, thick pieces. Place in large plastic bag. Repeat with red cabbage half. Add sliced red cabbage to sliced green cabbage in bag. Slice green onions diagonally, one at a time, from green tips to roots. Discard dried ends. Add to the cabbage. Shake and spin bag to mix greens. Empty greens into a large bowl. Shake dressing vigorously to mix, then pour 1/2 the dressing over the greens and mix with tongs to moisten greens. Add additional dressing as desired. Crumble ramen noodles evenly over the greens.

Dressing:

2 T. sesame seeds, toasted
2 T. slivered almonds, toasted
2 T. white sugar
3 T. rice vinegar
1/8 c. sesame oil
1/4 to 1/2 c. salad oil
1/2 t. pepper

Measure sesame seeds into a non-stick frying pan. Over a low flame, toast seeds until slightly brown. Remove from heat and let cool. Repeat these steps with the almonds. Over a low flame, heat sugar and rice vinegar until sugar is dissolved. Remove from heat. In a container that can be sealed and shaken, combine oils, pepper, cooled sesame seeds, almonds and the sugar solution.

Make a new Christmas bulb look more old-fashioned by covering it with a lace doily. Secure it with a length of ribbon tied around the top, hang on your tree.

Vegetable Garden Casserole

Kathy Grashoff
Ft. Wayne, IN

A delicious vegetable casserole.

4 c. zucchini, thinly sliced
2/3 c. onion, thinly sliced
2 c. tomato wedges
4 oz. green chilies, diced
1 c. tomato sauce
4 strips bacon, fried and crumbled
1-1/2 c. Provolone or Cheddar cheese, grated
1 c. cottage cheese
2 t. oregano or basil
1 t. garlic powder
1/2 t. salt
dash of pepper
1/4 c. bread crumbs
1/4 c. Parmesan cheese, grated

Butter a 3-quart casserole dish. In order given, layer 1/2 of each: zucchini, onion, tomatoes, chilies, tomato sauce, bacon, mixed cheeses and spices. Repeat. Top with crumbs and Parmesan cheese. Bake, covered, at 350 degrees for 25 minutes. Uncover and bake 10 minutes or longer.

Dip pretzel rods in semi-sweet chocolate and then roll them in sprinkled goodies...coconut, crushed nuts, cookie sprinkles, or small candies are all terrific!

Apricot Holiday Ham

Tami Bowman
Gooseberry Patch

A favorite for the buffet table.

5-lb. canned ham, fully cooked
whole cloves
18-oz. jar apricot preserves
2 t. cornstarch
1 t. orange peel, finely shredded
1/2 c. orange or pineapple juice
1/8 t. ground cinnamon
20-oz. can pineapple slices, drained

Place ham on a rack in a shallow baking pan. Score top of ham in a diamond pattern, making cuts about 1/4-inch deep. Stud with whole cloves. Insert a meat thermometer into center of ham. Bake at 325 degrees about 2 hours, or until thermometer registers 140 degrees. Combine apricot preserves and cornstarch. Stir in orange peel, orange or pineapple juice and ground cinnamon. Cook and stir until thickened and bubbly. Top ham with pineapple slices. Spoon some of the preserves mixture over the ham 2 or 3 times during the last 30 minutes of baking. Before serving, discard cloves and slice ham thinly. Serve with remaining sauce and pineapple slices. Serves 20.

Wrap your linen dinner napkins like little presents! Fold napkins into squares and trim with a bow...lovely!

Braised Chicken Breast

Yvonne Kuzmich
Huntsville, AL

Very elegant looking...and easy to prepare.

4 to 6 boneless chicken breasts
1 c. flour
salt & pepper to taste
2 to 4 T. butter
1/2 c. onions, diced
1 c. fresh or canned mushrooms, sliced
8-oz. can tomatoes, diced
1/2 c. chicken broth
2 T. prepared yellow mustard
1/2 pt. heavy whipping cream
Garnish: parsley

Dredge chicken in flour, salt and pepper mixture. Using an electric fry pan, brown chicken using butter. Add onions and mushrooms; cook until tender. Add diced tomatoes, chicken broth and mustard. Mix to blend. Simmer on low for 20 to 30 minutes. Add whipping cream mix to blend. Heat through. Garnish with chopped parsley. Serve over rice, noodles, or boiled potatoes.

"It is good to be children sometimes, and never better than at Christmas."

-Charles Dickens

Scallop & Shrimp with Linquine

Amy Biermann
Riverside, OH

Everyone will love this!

1/2 c. green onion, chopped
3 cloves garlic
3 T. olive oil
3 T. margarine
1 lb. fresh scallops
1 lb. med. shrimp
2 t. dry parsley
1 t. dry basil
1/2 t. crushed red pepper
10 oz. linguine
1/2 c. mushrooms, sliced
2 c. fresh pea pods
2 tomatoes, chopped

Cook onion, garlic, oil and margarine on medium-high heat for 5 minutes. Add scallops and shrimp; stir. Sprinkle in parsley, basil and crushed red pepper. Cook 3 to 4 minutes; add mushrooms, peapods and tomatoes. Cook until peapods are tender. Cook the linguine according to package directions; drain. Once the linguine is done, drain and add to the scallop mixture. Serve topped with Parmesan cheese.

You can find the most beautiful mismatched plates at yard sales. During the Christmas season use these special finds to give with your homemade treats from your kitchen. Your family and friends not only get to enjoy your goodies, but they can keep the beautiful plate as a reminder of your friendship!

Jeannine Johnson-Tatum, Wauchula, FL

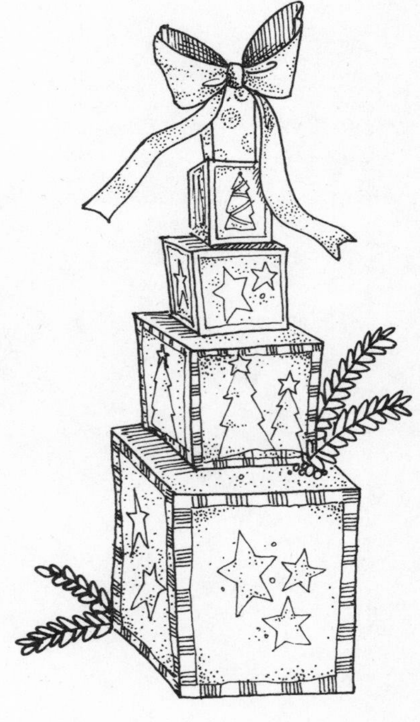

Carrot Cake & Brown Sugar Sauce

Gail Robinson
Logan, UT

Carrot cake with a warm, sweet sauce.

2 c. sugar
1/2 c. butter
2 eggs
3 c. apple, grated
1 c. carrots, grated

2 c. flour
2 t. baking soda
2 t. cinnamon
1 t. nutmeg
1/2 t. salt

Cream sugar and butter. Add eggs; beat until fluffy. Mix in apple and carrot. Sift dry ingredients together and add to creamed mixture. Bake in greased 13"x9" cake pan at 350 degrees for 30 to 45 minutes, until toothpick comes out clean. Serves 12. May be served warm or cold.

Brown Sugar Sauce:

4 c. boiling water
1-1/2 c. brown sugar
4 T. corn starch

1 t. vanilla
4 T. butter
1 t. nutmeg

Boil water in separate pan. Mix sugar and cornstarch in saucepan and add boiling water slowly. Bring to a boil, stirring constantly for 5 minutes. Remove from heat and add vanilla, butter and nutmeg. Serve warm.

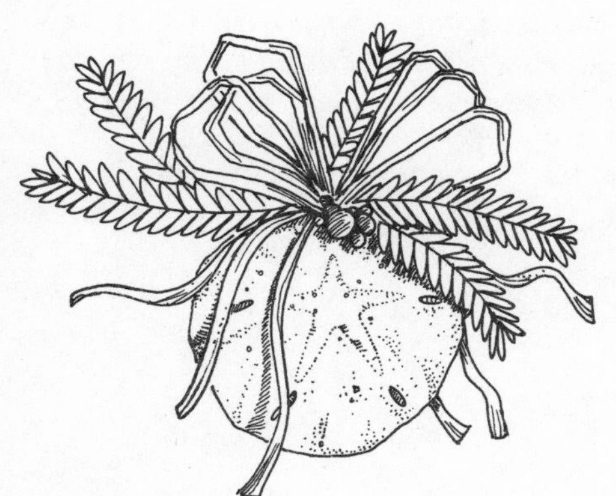

Place a fresh or dried artichoke in a small terra cotta pot. Tuck a candle in the middle...pretty at each place setting!

Liz Kenneweg, Gooseberry Patch

Spicy Pumpkin Cheesecake

Sharon Hall
Gooseberry Patch

A new twist on pumpkin pie!

1 egg yolk
graham cracker pie crust, extra large
2 8-oz. pkgs. cream cheese, softened
3/4 c. sugar
2 eggs
16-oz. can pumpkin
2 t. cinnamon
1/4 t. ginger
1/4 t. cloves
whipped cream

Beat egg yolk and brush on crust. Bake at 350 degrees for 5 minutes. Set aside. In a large mixing bowl, beat cream cheese, sugar and eggs on medium speed until smooth. Add pumpkin and spices; continue mixing until well blended. Spoon into pie crust and bake at 350 degrees until set, about 45 minutes. Cool, refrigerate several hours. Top with whipped cream.

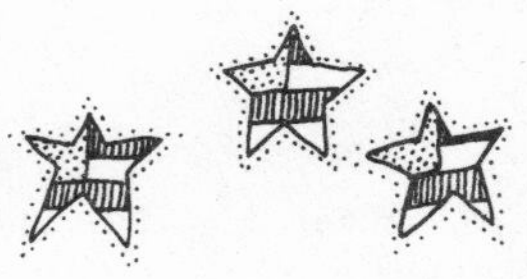

Before burning candles you've nestled in a votive cup or candle pan, spray the base with a little non-stick cooking spray so that the candles ease right out after burning!

Aleathea Searles-Millard, Houston, TX

English Trifle

Linda Desmond
Ontario, CA

Impressive looking!

4-oz. pkg. vanilla instant pudding
12-oz. tub whipped topping
1 angel food cake
2 10-oz. pkgs. frozen strawberries with juice, sliced

Mix the vanilla pudding and whipped topping together. Tear cake in small pieces and place some on the bottom of a clear, decorative bowl. Spoon pudding mixture over cake. Layer strawberries over pudding. Add another cake layer and continue layering pudding and strawberries. End with pudding mixture on top. Spoon a little strawberry mixture over the last pudding layer and swirl it around with a fork.

Need some ideas to help ease the post-Christmas depression? Decorate for winter! Save your snowmen and snow villages for use after Christmas. You can leave your evergreens around your mantels and windows, just change your holiday bows to blue, silver, or white. Hang snowflakes and leave your mini trees out to enjoy.

Jan Stafford, Chickamauga, CA

Southern Pecan Pie

Susan Bowman
Moline, IL

A perfect dessert for your holiday gathering.

3 eggs
2 T. butter, melted
2 T. flour
1/4 t. vanilla
1/8 t. salt
1/2 c. sugar
1-1/2 c. light corn syrup
1/2 c. pecans
1 unbaked pie shell

Beat eggs well then blend in butter, flour, vanilla, salt, sugar and syrup. Sprinkle whole pecans over bottom of pie shell then gently pour egg mixture over pecans. Bake at 425 degrees for 10 minutes. Reduce heat to 325 degrees and continue baking for an additional 40 minutes or until the middle is set.

Cranberry Sorbet with Lime

The Governor's Inn
Ludow, VT

Refreshing!

1-lb. can whole berry cranberry sauce
1 small container frozen limeade concentrate
3/4 c. champagne
2 egg whites
Garnish: lime slices, parsley

Place all ingredients in a food processor and whirl until completely blended. Pour into a metal cake pan and freeze until almost solid. Return to food processor and whip until frothy. Pour into a plastic freezer container and store until ready to use. Scoop into a beautiful footed compote and splash liberally with champagne. Serve at once garnished with a wheel of lime and parsley. Serves 12.

Recreate the joy of going to an old-fashioned candy store. Gather together several old-time canning jars and fill them will all sorts of wonderful holiday treats! Nestle among some greenery...a tempting display!

Stacey Spaseff, Lakewood, CA

Mom's Hermit Bars

Donna Bleistein
Berwick, PA

Enjoy these with a glass of cold milk.

1 c. margarine, softened
1-1/4 c. brown sugar
2 eggs
2 T. milk
2 c. flour
1/2 t. baking soda
1/2 t. nutmeg
1/2 t. cinnamon
1/2 t. allspice
1 c. raisins

Mix together margarine, brown sugar, eggs and milk. Sift together flour, baking soda, nutmeg, cinnamon and allspice. Combine mixtures and add raisins. Spread batter onto a greased 15"x10"x1" pan. Bake at 375 degrees for 20 minutes. Cool in pan. Cut into bars.

If you have college age children, purchase a big stocking and paint their college name on the front. Fill the stocking with things to make their room bright for the holidays...lights, ornaments, holiday music on CD or tape, and mini garlands. Tuck in some Christmas cookies for them to enjoy while they decorate!

Kathy Grashoff, Ft. Wayne, IN

Peppermint Cookie Canes

Kara Kimerline
Galion, OH

These are worth the extra time!

2 c. flour
1/2 c. sugar
1 c. margarine
1/4 c. milk
1/4 t. peppermint extract
1 c. rolled oats

Sift together flour and sugar. Cut in margarine until the mixture resembles coarse crumbs. Stir in milk and peppermint extract. Add oats. Mix well. Chill one to 2 hours. Divide dough into 4 equal parts, divide each part into 9 pieces. Roll each piece into a 6-inch rope about the size of a pencil. Shape into a candy cane and place on an ungreased cookie sheet. Bake at 375 degrees for 10 minutes. Cool. Frost with a thin powdered sugar icing. Before the icing is set, sprinkle with bands of red sugar to form stripes.

Tuck greenery, wooden spoons and a whisk inside a festive oven mitt. Top with a big bow...perfect for the cook on your gift list or to decorate your own kitchen!

Kathy Grashoff, Ft. Wayne, IN

Chocolate-Covered Cherry Cookies

Karen Stoner
Gooseberry Patch

These will be a favorite!

1-1/2 c. all-purpose flour
1/2 c. unsweetened cocoa powder
1/4 t. salt
1/4 t. baking powder
1/4 t. baking soda
1/2 c. butter, softened
1 c. sugar
1 egg
1-1/2 t. vanilla
10-oz. jar maraschino cherries (about 48)
6-oz. pkg. semi-sweet chocolate pieces
1/2 c. sweetened condensed milk

In a large bowl stir together flour, cocoa powder, salt, baking powder and baking soda. In mixing bowl, beat together butter and sugar on low speed until fluffy. Add egg and vanilla; beat well. Gradually add dry ingredients to creamed mixture; beat until well blended. Shape dough into one-inch balls; place on ungreased cookie sheet. Press down center of dough with thumb. Drain maraschino cherries, reserving juice. Place a cherry in the center of each cookie. In small saucepan, combine chocolate pieces and sweetened condensed milk. Heat until chocolate is melted. Stir in 4 teaspoons of the reserved cherry juice. Spoon one teaspoon of frosting over each cherry, spreading to cover cherry. Frosting may be thinned with additional cherry juice if necessary. Bake in 350 degree oven about 10 minutes or until done. Remove to wire rack; cool. Makes 48 cookies.

Have friends over to exchange homemade ornaments!

Grandmom's Soft Biscotti

Donna McGee
Dublin, PA

A family recipe made the old-fashioned way with lots of time and love. A wonderful Italian tradition!

4 lg. eggs
1-1/2 c. sugar
2 t. vanilla
1 c. shortening, melted
1/2 c. milk
6 c. all-purpose flour
2 T. baking powder
1 T. lemon juice
1 T. lemon zest

Beat the eggs until pale in color. Add sugar and vanilla; beat until mixture is thick. Add melted shortening and milk; mix well. Add flour and baking powder to the egg mixture. Add lemon juice and zest, mixing well. Wrap the dough in plastic wrap and refrigerate until firm. Preheat oven to 350 degrees. Lightly grease cookie sheets. Pinch enough dough to make walnut-sized balls. On a floured surface, roll to make round; flatten slightly and place on the cookie sheet. Bake at 350 degrees for 20 minutes, or until just golden in color. Place on wire racks, frost while still warm.

Frosting:

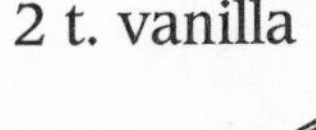

1-1/2 c. powdered sugar
1/4 c. milk
2 t. vanilla

Combine ingredients and drizzle over warm cookies. Allow frosting to set before storing.

Curl up under a quilt and enjoy the wonderful variety of seasonal books and stories!

Chocolate Oat Chip Jar Cookies

Kristi Cruz
Fresno, CA

Layer the dry ingredients in a jar...a perfect gift!

1/4 c. instant chocolate drink mix
3/4 c. flour
1/4 t. salt
1/2 t. baking soda
1/2 c. plus 1 t. brown sugar
1/4 c. sugar
1-1/4 c. instant oats
1 c. chocolate chips
1/2 c. margarine
1 egg
1 T. milk
1 t. vanilla extract

Layer first 8 dry ingredients in order in a wide-mouth one-quart canning jar; pack tightly so all ingredients will fit. Tighten the jar lid securely. Before giving as a gift, attach a festive card or label with the remaining ingredients listed and these instructions.

In a large mixing bowl, blend margarine, egg, milk and vanilla with dry ingredients. Drop by rounded tablespoons onto an ungreased cookie sheet. Bake at 375 degrees for 10 minutes for a chewy cookie, or 13 minutes for a crisper cookie. Enjoy!

To add Christmas cheer to your gathering, roll silverware in holiday napkins, fasten with a red bow tied around a candy cane or jingle bell.

Nancy Molldrem, Eau Claire, WI

Chocolate Gingerbread Cookies

Mildred Bright
Riverdale, MD

Easy and delightful!

1/2 c. molasses
1/4 c. sugar
3 T. butter
1 T. milk
2 c. flour
1/2 t. baking soda
1/2 t. nutmeg
1/2 t. cinnamon
1/2 t. cloves
1/2 t. ginger
3 T. water

Heat molasses to boiling. Reduce heat to medium and add sugar, butter and milk. Stir until butter melts. In a large bowl mix in dry ingredients with molasses mixture, blend well. Add water. Roll to 1/4-inch thickness, and cut with your favorite cookie cutter. Spray cookie sheet lightly with non-stick vegetable spray; bake at 350 degrees for 5 to 7 minutes.

Icing:

8 oz. chocolate bits, melted
1/3 c. warm milk

Stir chocolate bits and warm milk together until smooth and drizzle over cookies.

Annie's Soft Molasses Cookies

Madge Bowman
Shreve, OH

Madge's aunt used to make these yummy cookies 4 inches in size and bake them in a woodstove!

1 c. sugar
1 c. shortening, melted
1 c. light molasses
1 egg, beaten
4 t. baking soda
2/3 c. hot water
1 T. vanilla
5 c. flour
1-1/2 t. cream of tartar
1-1/2 t. ginger
1-1/2 t. cinnamon
1/2 t. cloves
3/4 t. salt

Mix sugar, shortening and molasses. Add beaten egg. Dissolve soda in the hot water and add vanilla; mix well and set aside. Sift together flour, cream of tartar, spices and salt. Combine thoroughly with molasses mixture. Chill dough for at least one hour. Roll 1/4-inch thick and cut out with round cutter. Place on greased baking sheet. Bake at 375 degrees for 8 to 10 minutes.

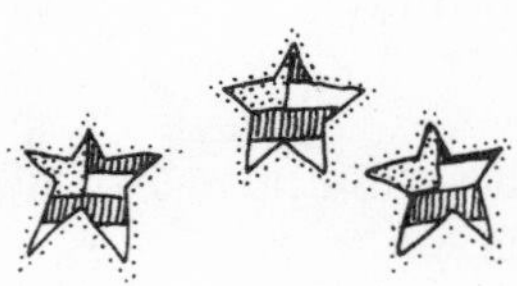

Wear something festive during the holidays! Jingle bells on shoe laces, Christmas balls for earrings, glittery sweaters, colorful socks, or a Santa hat...all will lift your spirit as well as those around you!

Cranberry Date Squares

Leona Rutledge
W. Wareham, MA

You'll be asked to share this recipe!

12-oz. pkg. fresh cranberries
8-oz. pkg. dates, chopped and pitted
1 t. vanilla
2 c. flour
2 c. quick-cooking oats
1-1/2 c. brown sugar, packed
1/2 t. baking soda
1/4 t. salt
1 c. butter, softened

In a medium saucepan, combine cranberries and dates; cook, covered over low heat for 15 minutes until cranberries start to pop and are soft. Stirring frequently, let cool off the stove; then add vanilla. Set aside. In a large bowl stir together flour, oats, brown sugar, baking soda, salt. Add to softened butter, stir until well blended; mixture will have a crumbly texture. Pat half of the mix on the bottom of a 13"x9"x2" pan. Bake in 350 degree oven for 8 minutes. Let sit for a few minutes to firm. Carefully spread cranberry and date filling over the baked oats. Try not to go to the very edge of the baked oats. Then sprinkle the crumbly oat mixture over the filling, pat gently and bake for 20 to 22 minutes, until very light golden brown, do not over bake. Cool completely.

Orange Glaze Topping:

2 c. powdered sugar, sifted
1/2 t. vanilla
3 to 5 T. orange juice

Stir together powdered sugar, and vanilla. Add orange juice until mixture reaches a drizzle consistency.

Build a fire in the fireplace to enjoy all day!

Chocolate Marshmallow Cookies

Margaret Scoresby
Mount Vernon, OH

You'll love these!

1/2 c. butter
1 c. sugar
1 egg
1/4 c. milk
1 t. vanilla
1/3 c. cocoa
1-3/4 c. flour
1/2 t. soda
1/2 t. salt
16 to 18 marshmallows

Cream together butter and sugar. Beat in egg, milk and vanilla. Add dry ingredients and mix well. Drop by teaspoonfuls on ungreased cookie sheet and bake at 350 degrees for 8 minutes. Remove from oven and top each cookie with a marshmallow half. Bake 2 more minutes. Remove and cool slightly.

Frosting:

6 T. butter
2 T. cocoa
1/4 c. milk
1-3/4 c. powdered sugar
1/2 t. vanilla
pecans, halved

Boil butter, cocoa and milk together for one minute. Cool slightly; add sugar and vanilla; beat well. Drizzle one tablespoon over each cookie and top with a pecan half.

"...seek peace and comfort in the joyful simplicities."

-Woman's Home Companion, 1935

Grandma's Scottish Shortbread

Stephanie Whitehead
Trappe, MD

Enjoy these with a cup of tea.

4 c. all-purpose flour
8 T. sweet rice flour
1 c. white sugar
powdered sugar
1 lb. butter

Sift first 3 ingredients together in a large bowl. Cut butter into dry ingredients with a pastry blender. Divide dough in 4 even parts. Working with one quarter at a time, coat one quarter of the dough with powdered sugar and lay plastic wrap over it. Roll out dough 1/4-inch thick. Cut dough with cookie cutter of your choice. Repeat with remaining quarters. Prick each cookie several times with a fork. Bake at 350 degrees for 10 minutes, until just golden. Cool on wire racks, then store in tins.

Collect poetry and sayings from old Christmas cards. They're perfect if you design your own needlework or greeting cards.

Chocolate Raspberry Truffles

Patti Kachmar
Kingston, PA

Terrific for gift-giving!

12-oz. bag chocolate-raspberry chips
5-1/2 T. butter
3 T. heavy cream
powdered sugar

Place first 3 ingredients in a microwave-safe bowl. Melt 1-1/2 to 2 minutes. Stir until creamy and combined. Mixture will be thin. Freeze exactly one hour. Using melon ball scooper, or a tablespoon, drop and roll in powdered sugar. Store in refrigerator until ready to serve.

Enjoy a hayride this Christmas! Sing songs, bundle up under cozy quilts, come home to some hot cider or cocoa!

Cheery Cherry Cheesecake Bars

Sharon Harris
Herndon, PA

A family favorite passed down from Sharon's Grandma Flora.

1/3 c. butter
1/3 c. brown sugar, firmly packed
1 c. all-purpose flour

Preheat oven to 350 degrees. In medium mixing bowl, cream butter, brown sugar and flour. Mix well. Reserve 1/2 cup crumb mixture for top. Press remaining crumb mixture into 8" square baking pan. Bake in center of oven for 10 to 12 minutes, cool while preparing filling.

Filling:

8 oz. cream cheese, softened
1/4 c. sugar
1 egg
1 T. lemon juice
1/2 c. maraschino cherries, chopped

Beat cream cheese, sugar, egg and lemon juice until fluffy (one or 2 minutes). Stir in the cherries. Spread filling over baked crust. Sprinkle reserved crumb mixture over top. Bake again, 18 to 20 minutes or until the filling is set and top is lightly brown. Cool and store in refrigerator. Makes 32 to 36 bars.

Start a Santa collection!

Grandma Miller's Nutmeg Logs

Jenny Miller
Hollywood, FL

You'll want more than just one!

1 egg, slightly beaten
1 c. butter, softened
2 t. vanilla extract
2 t. rum extract
3/4 c. sugar
1 t. nutmeg
3 c. flour

Preheat oven to 350 degrees. Cream together egg, butter, vanilla, rum extract and sugar. Add nutmeg and flour to creamed ingredients. Divide dough to workable size, roll into long strips, cut to about 1-1/2 inch length. Place on ungreased cookie sheet. They can be packed close together as they will not rise. Bake at 350 degrees for 10 to 15 minutes.

Frosting:

3 T. butter, room temperature
1/2 t. vanilla extract
1 t. rum extract
2-1/2 c. powdered sugar
nutmeg

Mix ingredients together until desired consistency. After cookies have cooled, frost each, then run the tines of a fork across frosting to resemble a log. Sprinkle with nutmeg.

Take a tray of cookies, basket of fruit, or homemade bread to a nursing home, an elderly neighbor, or a friend who needs cheering. Stay to visit awhile.

Apricot Bars

Lesa Lafferty
Indiahoma, OK

These cookies refrigerate well.

3/4 c. butter
1 c. sugar
1/2 t. vanilla
1 egg
1/2 t. salt
2 c. flour
1-1/2 c. coconut
8-oz. jar apricot preserves
1/2 c. pecans, chopped

Cream the butter and sugar. Add vanilla, egg, salt, flour and coconut. Mix well. Spread 3/4 of the mixture in a greased 11"x7" oven-proof glass dish. Spread preserves on top. Combine the remaining quarter of the mixture and nuts. Crumble on top of the preserves. Bake at 350 degrees for 40 to 45 minutes, until golden. Cut into bars while still warm. Makes 20 bars.

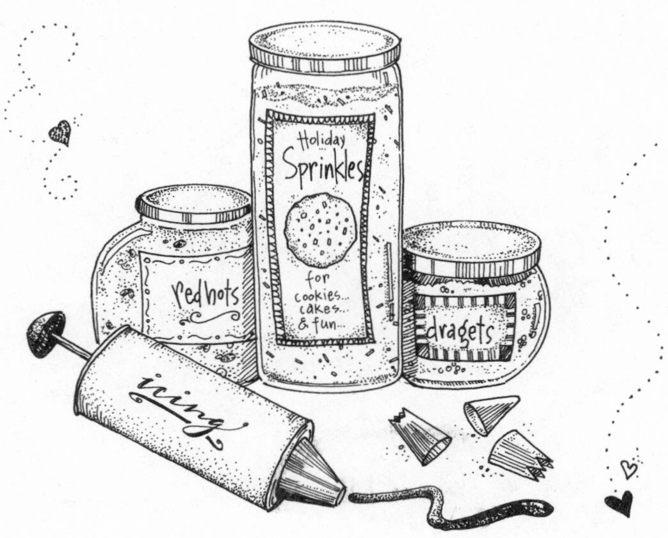

The glow from a votive candle looks lovely when you sit it behind a square of glass block. Easily found at most home supply centers, glass blocks can also be stacked with a votive placed behind each one.

Debbie Wakeland, Georgetown, KY

Peanut Butter Surprise Cookies

Jennifer Kane
Lebanon, PA

A burst of peanut butter flavor in each bite!

24 miniature peanut butter cups
1-1/2 c. light brown sugar, firmly packed
3/4 c. creamy peanut butter
1/2 c. shortening
3 T. milk
1 T. vanilla
1 egg
1-3/4 c. all-purpose flour
3/4 t. baking soda
3/4 t. salt

Remove wrappers from peanut butter cups. Cut candy into quarters. Combine brown sugar, peanut butter, shortening, milk and vanilla in large bowl. Beat at medium speed until well blended. Add egg. Beat until blended. Combine flour, baking soda and salt. Add to creamed mixture at low speed. Mix until blended. Stir in candy pieces. Drop by teaspoonful 2 to 3 inches apart. Bake at 375 degrees for 7 to 8 minutes. Cool 2 minutes and remove from sheets. Makes 3 dozen cookies.

Decorate the top of pinecones with berries, nuts, raffia and other natural gatherings. Hang or pile in a basket for true country charm.

Evelyn Bruce, St.Louis, MO

Cocoa Bars

Marilyn Welde
Pine Grove, CA

Wrap up some to share with a neighbor.

1/2 c. butter
2 c. sugar
2 t. vanilla
4 eggs
1/2 c. milk
2 c. flour, sifted
4 T. cocoa
1/2 t. salt
1 c. walnuts, chopped

Cream butter to soften. Gradually add sugar and vanilla, creaming well. Beat in eggs, one at a time, stir in milk. Sift together dry ingredients. Stir into creamed mixture. Add nuts. Spread into greased 15"x12" pan. Bake at 375 degrees for 20 to 25 minutes. Frost immediately.

Frosting:

3 T. cocoa
2 T. milk
1-1/3 c. powdered sugar, sifted
1/4 c. butter

Blend all ingredients and frost cookies immediately after baking. Cool and cut in bars after approximately one hour. Makes 4 dozen.

Cherry Bonbon Cookies

Flo Burtnett
Gage, OK

A family recipe that's over 30 years old.

24 maraschino cherries
1/2 c. margarine, softened
3/4 c. powdered sugar, sifted
1-1/2 c. all-purpose flour
1/8 t. salt
2 T. milk
1 t. vanilla

Drain cherries. Reserve 1/4 cup of juice for glaze and set aside. Beat margarine until creamy. Gradually add powdered sugar, beating well. Stir in flour, salt, milk and vanilla. Mix well. Shape in 24 balls. Press each ball around a cherry, covering it completely. Place on ungreased cookie sheets. Bake at 350 degrees for 18 to 20 minutes. Transfer to wire racks and cool completely. Sprinkle with powdered sugar and drizzle with cherry glaze.

Glaze:

2 T. margarine, melted
2 c. powdered sugar, sifted
1/4 c. reserved cherry juice

Mix margarine, powdered sugar and cherry juice. Place in a small zipping plastic bag and seal. To drizzle, snip a tiny hole at one corner of bag and gently squeeze.

Place a candle clip with a lighted candle on the edge of dessert plates when serving your favorite holiday dessert.

Judi Mohr
Plymouth, MN

Christmas Wreath Cookies

Dianne Wentz
Duluth, MN

A very festive cookie!

1/2 c. butter
4 c. miniature marshmallows
1/4 t. green food coloring
1/2 t. vanilla
1/4 t. almond extract
3-1/2 c. corn flake cereal
red cinnamon candies

Melt butter and marshmallows in double boiler or over low heat. Add green food coloring, vanilla, almond and stir well. Add cereal. Drop one spoonful onto wax paper, foil or greased cookie sheet. Grease fingers well and shape into a wreath, insert your finger in center and shape. Decorate with candies while sticky and warm. Repeat. For easier shaping, keep mixture in pan warm. Makes about 24 wreaths.

Paint wooden clothes pins in festive colors and lightly sprinkle with glitter. Use them to hang Christmas cards to garlands or clip lights to your tree.

Aleathea Searles-Millard, Houston, TX

Surprise Cherry Balls

Shirll Kosmal
Gooseberry Patch

You can cut these in half to serve...they look great!

1/4 c. butter, softened
1/2 c. peanut butter
2 c. powdered sugar
1 T. milk
1 jar maraschino cherries, well drained
5 squares semi-sweet chocolate
2 c. walnuts, chopped

Cream butter and peanut butter. Add sugar gradually, blend in milk. Shape one heaping teaspoon of this mixture around each cherry. Melt chocolate over low heat. Dip balls in the chocolate, roll in chopped nuts and refrigerate or freeze to keep firm.

A Christmas tree in the kitchen is a cheerful and unexpected surprise. It's very relaxing to sit down for dinner and to enjoy the twinkling lights.!

Balynda Elkins, Paulding, OH

One Cup of Everything Cookies

Claddagh Inn
Hendersonville, NC

Add any of your favorites!

1 c. sugar
1 c. brown sugar
1 c. margarine
1 egg
3-1/2 c. flour
1 t. baking soda
1 t. cream of tartar
1 t. vanilla
1 c. instant oatmeal, uncooked
1 c. crisped rice cereal
1 c. chocolate chips

Cream first 4 ingredients. Add remaining ingredients until dough is formed. Roll into one-inch balls and place on a cookie sheet. Flatten balls with a fork. Bake at 350 degrees for 10 minutes.

Leave a plate of cookies on a friend's car seat...what a pleasant surprise!

Crabmeat Dunk

The Governor's Inn
Ludlow, VT

Serves a house full!

1/2 lb. cream cheese
3 T. onion, chopped
3 T. horseradish
6 T. chili sauce
1-1/2 c. sour cream
5 drops hot sauce
2-1/2 lb. fresh crabmeat

Combine all of the ingredients, except crabmeat, and process in a food processor until well blended. Fold in crabmeat. Serve with crackers or crisp vegetables.

"And it was said of him that he knew how to keep Christmas well, if any man possessed the knowledge. And so, Tiny Tim observed, God bless us everyone!"
-Charles Dickens, A Christmas Carol

Christmas Shrimp Dip

Sandy Wisneski
Ripon, WI

You can substitute lobster or crab for the shrimp and bleu cheese makes a tasty difference when substituted for cream cheese!

3-oz. pkg. cream cheese, room temperature
1 T. mayonnaise
1 c. shrimp, minced
1/4 t. Worcestershire sauce
2 t. onion, grated
2 t. parsley, chopped
1-1/2 t. lemon juice
1/4 t. salt
3 drops hot pepper sauce

Mix cream cheese with mayonnaise. Add remaining ingredients and blend thoroughly. Allow mixture to chill for one hour so flavors will blend. Serve with crackers or potato chips. Makes 3/4 cup.

Remove the glass from an old barn window and decorate the frame with lots of evergreens, grapevine and red berries. Hang an old pair of skates over the top and you're ready to hang your masterpiece for everyone to see!

Missy Volkmann
Sauk Centre, MN

Weber Duck

Susan Smith
Walnutport, PA

No one knows where the name came from, but it's so tasty a name isn't necessary!

4-oz. pkg. bleu cheese
3-oz. pkg. cream cheese
2 T. onion, grated or chopped
6-oz. jar pimento spread or dip
1 t. Worcestershire sauce

Mash bleu and cream cheese with fork. Add onion. Mix thoroughly and form small cake. Put in freezer or refrigerator until firm. Mix pimento together with Worcestershire sauce and spread over bleu cheese mixture.

Cookie tins are perfect for packing fragile ornaments safely away.

Pam's Pineapple Cheeseball

Pam Marshall
Gooseberry Patch

You'll be surprised at how good these unusual combinations are!

2 8-oz. pkgs. cream cheese
16-oz. can crushed pineapple
1/4 c. green pepper, chopped
1 T. onion, chopped
1 t. salt

Soften cream cheese. Drain crushed pineapple. Mix together all ingredients and chill for one hour. Can be used as a spread or rolled into a ball.

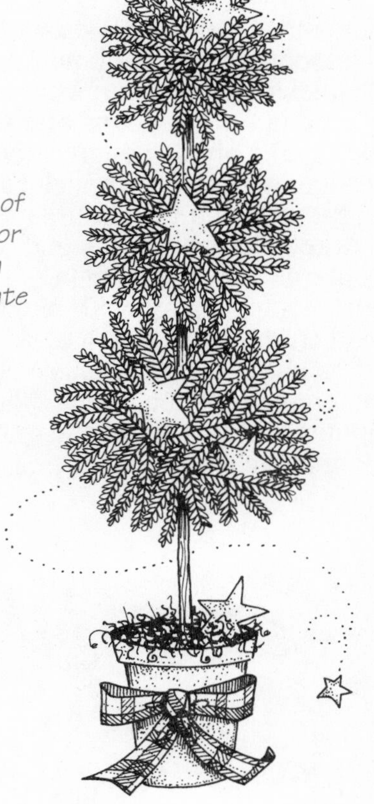

Choose a gift wrap theme for each member of your family...angels, Santas, holiday plaid, or gingerbread men are just right. Wrap each person's gift in "their" paper and you eliminate the need for gift tags!

Harriett Heppard, Drexel Hill, PA

Mushroom Strudel

The Governor's Inn
Ludlow, VT

The "most requested" recipe of The Governor's Inn.

6 c. mushrooms, top and stems, minced
1 t. salt
1/4 t. curry powder
6 T. sherry
4 T. shallots, chopped
1/2 c. plus 4 T. sweet unsalted butter
1 c. sour cream
1 c. plus 3 T. dry bread crumbs
1 pkg. frozen phyllo dough, thawed
Garnish: sour cream and parsley

Sauté mushrooms with seasonings, sherry and shallots in 4 tablespoons butter until mushrooms are wilted and liquid is gone. This will take about 60 minutes over low flame. Allow to cool. Add sour cream and 3 tablespoons of dry bread crumbs. Refrigerate overnight. Unwrap the phyllo dough carefully. Place a sheet of dough on a large breadboard. Brush with melted butter and sprinkle with bread crumbs. Repeat until you have four layers. Spoon half of the mushroom mixture onto one narrow end of the dough. Turn long sides of dough in about one inch to seal filling, then roll dough up much like a jelly roll. Brush completed roll with remaining melted butter and sprinkle with bread crumbs. Place on a cookie sheet that has been lightly greased. With a sharp knife, score each roll to serve 6. Repeat above process using remaining mushroom filling. Bake at 375 degrees for 40 minutes. Cut into slices and garnish each with a small dollop of sour cream and chopped parsley. Serve hot. Yields 12 slices.

Stencil holiday greetings on a large burlap sack, tie with a raffia bow...perfect for holding a large or bulky gift.

Dropped Tea Cakes

Rosa Strickland
Bradley, AR

This recipes makes 6 dozen delicious tea cakes...perfect for an open house!

1 c. butter, softened
2-1/4 c. sugar
4 eggs
4-1/2 c. flour
1 t. baking soda
1 t. baking powder
1/2 t. nutmeg
1/4 c. buttermilk
1 t. lemon extract
1 t. vanilla extract
1 t. almond extract

Cream butter. Gradually add sugar, beating well at medium speed. Add eggs, beating well. Combine flour, baking soda, baking powder and nutmeg. Add to creamed mixture alternately with buttermilk, mixing well. Stir in flavors. Drop dough by tablespoonfuls onto greased cookie sheets. Bake at 375 degrees for 8 to 10 minutes, or until lightly browned. Cool. Yields 6 dozen.

In a pinch for a table cloth? Buy two yards of holiday fabric and finish the edges. In no time you have a table topper!

Ann Fehr, Trappe, PA

Cranberry-Almond Punch

Susan Kennedy
Gooseberry Patch

A refreshing and colorful punch.

1 can jellied cranberry sauce
2-1/4 c. water
1/2 c. lemon juice
3/4 c. orange juice
1 t. almond extract
1 c. ginger ale, chilled

With fork, crush cranberry sauce; beat smooth with hand beater, then beat in water, lemon juice, orange juice and almond. Chill. At serving time, stir in ginger ale. Garnish glasses with lemon slices and mint. Serves 4.

Use poly-fil to resemble mounds of snow all around your home! Mound it at the bottom of your Christmas tree, around your Christmas village, and even on window sills. No matter where you live you can have a white Christmas!

Phyllis Stout, East Palatka, FL

Yuletime Spread

Pam Hansberger
Norwalk, OH

Easily doubled for gift giving!

1 med. onion
2 T. prepared horseradish
1 t. dill
1 dash hot pepper sauce
8 oz. cream cheese, softened
1 lb. braunsweiger
3 T. dried parsley or chives
1/4 c. coconut, shredded
1 red cherry

In a food processor or by hand, finely mince onion. Mix in horseradish, dill and hot sauce. Fold in cream cheese and braunsweiger. Mix until well blended. Chill overnight. Just before serving, shape spread into a cone shape. Roll cone in parsley or chives, your cone should now look like a Christmas tree. Spread coconut on a small plate and place your cone in the middle. Using a tooth pick, put a cherry on top. Serve with crackers or toast points.

Place a votive on an old-fashioned tin saucer and surround it with peppermint candies...lovely!

Penny McShane, Lombard, IL

Shrimp Creole

Debra Arnold
Easton, MO

To save time, peel the shrimp the night before your open house.

1/4 c. bacon grease
1/4 c. flour
1-1/2 c. onion, chopped
1 c. green onions, chopped
1 c. celery & leaves, chopped
1 c. bell pepper, chopped
2 cloves garlic
6-oz. can tomato paste
16-oz. can chopped tomatoes with liquid
8-oz. can tomato sauce
1 c. water
5 t. salt
1 t. pepper
1/2 t. red pepper
3 bay leaves
1 t. sugar
1 t. Worcestershire sauce
1 t. lemon juice
1/2 c. parsley, chopped
hot pepper sauce to taste
10 lbs. shrimp, shelled and deveined

Make a dark brown roux out of bacon grease and flour. Add onions and all ingredients except shrimp. Add shrimp after the sauce has simmered one hour, remove from heat then let sit one additional hour. Shrimp will continue to cook in hot sauce. Serve over rice. Serves 12 to 15.

Some of the best things about winter...frosty nights, moonlight on the snow, a crackling fire, snowmen, curling up under a quilt and the wintry smell of wood smoke.

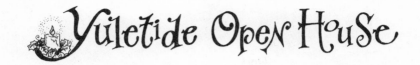

Whiskey Kielbasa

Tammy Del Fino
Attleboro, MA

A new addition to your buffet table.

3 to 5 lb. kielbasa
1 c. whiskey
1 c. catsup
1 c. brown sugar

Boil kielbasa 20 minutes, slice and set aside. Boil whiskey, catsup and brown sugar over low heat until mixture is thoroughly combined. Pour mix into a slow cooker along with cooked kielbasa. Cook for 3 to 4 hours.

Take a few of your favorite pictures to a copy center and have color copies made and blown up to letter-size. These make wonderful holiday stationery to send to family and friends.

Aleathea Searles-Millard
Houston, TX

Seafood Casserole

Leslie Carpenter
Richmond, VA

Delicious!

1/2 c. green pepper, chopped
1/2 c. onion, chopped
1/2 c. celery, chopped
8 oz. fresh mushrooms, sliced
1/2 c. margarine
2/3 c. flour
1/2 t. garlic, minced
1/2 t. salt
1/4 t. paprika
dash red pepper
10-oz. can cream of shrimp soup
2 c. milk
16 oz. crabmeat
2 lbs. raw shrimp, peeled
8-oz. can water chestnuts
2 T. butter, softened
1/2 c. sharp Cheddar cheese, grated
1/2 c. fresh bread crumbs

Sauté pepper, onion, celery and mushrooms in margarine. Stir in flour and cook one minute. Add seasonings. Stir in soup and milk. Continue to stir until thickened. Combine crabmeat, shrimp and water chestnuts in a 2-quart casserole. Pour sauce over seafood mixture. Combine butter, cheese and crumbs. Sprinkle over casserole. Bake at 350 degrees for 30 to 35 minutes. Serves 8 to 10.

Old-fashioned Christmas ornaments are so pretty in a cut glass bowl or vase. Even the not-so-perfect ones are charming.

Evelyn Bruce, St. Louis, MO

Cranberry Glazed Meatballs

Penny Pickett
Lacey, WA

The cranberries add a new twist!

2 lbs. lean ground beef
1 c. corn flake cereal, crushed
1/2 c. parsley flakes
2 eggs, slightly beaten
2 T. soy sauce
1/4 t. pepper
1 t. onion, minced
1/3 c. catsup
16-oz. can jellied cranberry sauce
12-oz. bottle chili sauce
2 T. brown sugar
1 t. lemon juice

Mix beef, corn flakes, parsley, eggs, soy sauce, pepper, onion and catsup with a fork. Gently form into one-inch balls. Place in large glass baking pan sprayed with non-stick vegetable spray. Refrigerate while making sauce. Heat cranberry sauce, chili sauce, brown sugar and lemon juice in pan. Mix well as you stir. Pour hot sauce over meatballs. Bake at 350 degrees for one hour. Serve as a meal over rice or noodles, or as an appetizer.

Fill an empty oatmeal container with yummy homemade oatmeal cookies. Give to a friend...just because.

Aleathea Searles-Millard, Houston, TX

Stuffed Mushroom Caps

Lisa Miller
Lorain, OH

This appetizer can be prepared 3 days ahead of your open house!

25 fresh mushrooms
1 small onion, chopped
1/4 c. margarine
1 to 1-1/2 c. mozzarella cheese, shredded
3-oz. jar bacon bits
1/2 to 1 c. fine dry bread crumbs

Rinse mushrooms and pat dry. Remove stems; set caps aside. Chop stems finely. Sauté with onion and margarine in skillet. Remove from heat. Stir in cheese, bacon bits and bread crumbs, mixing well. Spoon mixture into mushroom caps. Place on baking sheet. Bake at 350 degrees for 12 to 15 minutes or until lightly browned. May store, covered, in refrigerator for 3 days before baking.

Get your friends together for a night of baking and cookie decorating. Give your finished goodies to the fire or police department staffs who have to work Christmas day.

Holiday Hamballs

Jackie Crough
Salina, KS

Easily served in your slow cooker.

1-1/2 lbs. ground ham
1 lb. ground pork
2 eggs
1 c. milk
1-1/2 c. cracker crumbs
1 c. brown sugar
1/2 c. vinegar
1 T. mustard
1/2 c. water

Combine ham, pork, eggs, milk and crumbs to make 24 balls. In a saucepan, cook brown sugar, vinegar, mustard and water for approximately 5 minutes. Pour over hamballs. Bake at 350 degrees for one to 2 hours, basting occasionally.

Throw a caroling party! Bring along the words to your favorite carols and visit your neighbors, a nursing home or hospital. End the evening with cocoa and cookies at your home.

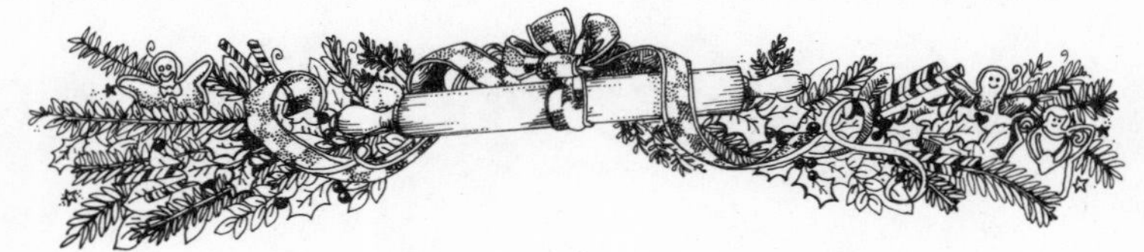

Apple Cake

Pam Hilton
Centerburg, OH

Drizzle warm vanilla sauce over cake slices.

1 c. oil
2 c. sugar
2 eggs
1 t. vanilla
1 t. salt
1 t. baking soda
2 t. baking powder
2-1/2 c. flour
3 c. apples, chopped

Beat oil, sugar, eggs and vanilla together. Blend in dry ingredients, then stir in apples. Pour into a lightly oiled 13"x9" pan.

Topping:

1/3 c. brown sugar
1 t. cinnamon
1/2 c. nuts, chopped

Combine topping ingredients and sprinkle over cake. Bake cake at 350 degrees for 40 to 45 minutes. Remove from oven; serve warm with vanilla sauce.

Vanilla Sauce:

1/2 c. butter
1-1/2 c. whipping cream
1 c. sugar
2 T. flour
2 t. vanilla

Blend first four ingredients together well and cook in a saucepan over medium heat, stirring often, until thickened. Add vanilla and stir.

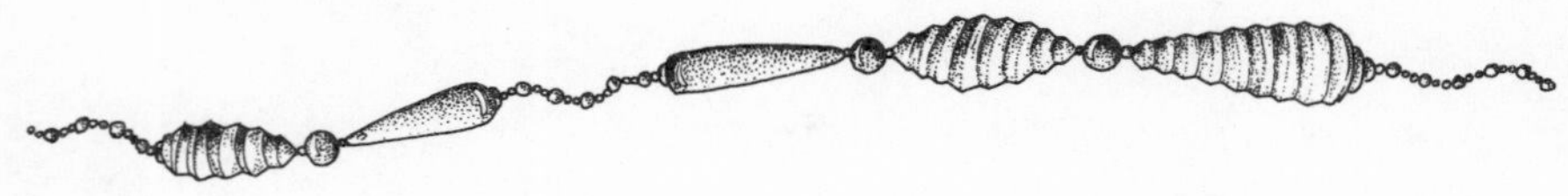

Christmas Creame

The Governor's Inn
Ludlow, VT

A sensational punch bowl treat!

3 eggs
1 c. heavy cream
14-oz. can sweetened condensed milk
3 T. chocolate syrup
1/2 t. pure vanilla extract
1/2 t. coconut extract
Garnish: nutmeg

Mix all ingredients in a blender. Serve chilled in a punch bowl, garnished with sprinkles of nutmeg. Serve on your buffet...delicious enjoyed with plates of rich, chewy chocolate brownies and slices of old-fashioned sponge cake. Serves 10.

Place a wooden nativity scene on an outdoor bench. Surround it with cedar cuttings and add a soft spotlight for a warm glow. It's a wonderful addition to your decorations and this beautiful season.

Linda Thompson, Mt. Juliet, TN

Marshmallow Creme Mocha

Linda Webb
Delaware, OH

Serve with a cinnamon stick.

2 t. instant coffee
2 t. unsweetened cocoa powder
4 t. sugar
1 t. cinnamon
1-3/4 c. milk, divided
1/4 c. whipped cream or 1/4 c. marshmallow creme

In a medium mixing bowl, combine instant coffee, cocoa, sugar and cinnamon. Stir in 1/4 cup milk and blend until thick. In a saucepan, scald remaining milk, add to coffee mixture. Whisk until blended and a froth forms. Pour mixture into cups. Top each with a dollop of whipped cream or marshmallow creme. Serve immediately.

"Christmas, my child is love in action. Every time we love, every time we give, it's Christmas."

-Dale Evans

Creme Cocoa Punch

Carol Bull
Gooseberry Patch

This will be a hit at your gathering!

4-oz. jar instant coffee
4 c. boiling water
4 c. sugar
1 gal. chocolate ice cream, divided
1 gal. vanilla ice cream, divided
1 gal. milk, divided

In a large container, dissolve instant coffee powder in boiling water. Add sugar; stir until sugar and coffee dissolve. Refrigerate covered, overnight to let flavors blend. To serve, put half of the chocolate ice cream and half of the vanilla ice cream in a large punch bowl. Add half of the chilled coffee mixture and half of the milk. Stir to partly melt the ice creams. Midway through the party, combine remaining chilled coffee mixture, remaining chocolate and vanilla ice creams and remaining milk in another container. Use to replenish the punch bowl.

Add a teaspoon of red and green sprinkle sugar to your bowl of granulated sugar...it gives a fun look to your coffee tray!

Judi Mohr, Plymouth, MN

Sweet Almond Coffee

Vickie

Enjoy this sweet cocoa-almond blend on a frosty night.

1/4 c. unsweetened cocoa powder
1/4 c. instant coffee powder
1/2 c. sugar
1/4 c. plus 2 T. finely ground almonds, divided
1/4 t. salt
2 t. non-dairy, powdered coffee creamer
4-1/2 c. milk
whipped cream

In an electric blender, combine cocoa, instant coffee, sugar, 1/4 cup ground almonds, salt and coffee creamer. Cover and blend on high speed for 10 seconds. Heat milk in a 2 quart saucepan. Do not boil. Add cocoa mixture to hot milk; stir to combine. Pour into mugs. Top each serving with a dollop of whipped cream and a sprinkling of the remaining 2 tablespoons of the ground almonds.

Simple can be better...hang a grapevine wreath from your porch beam or rafter. Intertwine it with bittersweet and hang an old railroad lantern on the same nail so it can be seen in the center.

The Governor's Hot Buttered Coffee

Governor's Inn
Ludlow, VT

Perfect for a dessert party!

1/2 stick sweet, unsalted butter
2 c. dark brown sugar
1/4 t. cinnamon,
1/4 t. nutmeg
1/4 t. allspice, ground
1/4 t. cloves, ground
1 oz. dark rum (optional)
1 oz. heavy cream
freshly brewed coffee, strong and very hot
Garnish: whipped cream

Cream butter and sugar and blend in spices. Refrigerate in a jar until ready to use. This will keep indefinitely. When ready to serve, place a scant tablespoon of the spice mixture in a 10-ounce clear glass, heat-proof mug. Add rum and heavy cream. Fill each cup with coffee. Garnish with a spritz of whipped cream. Recipe makes 20 servings.

Decorate with lots of candles...tall, fat, short! Set tea lights in bowls of coarse salt, or fill an empty fireplace with candles! Create magic for your coffee and dessert party, light your entire house by candlelight!

Brown Sugar Coffee

Jo Ann

You can substitute milk for cream if you'd like.

1 c. hot, brewed coffee
2 T. heavy cream
2 T. dark brown sugar
1/2 t. vanilla
1/4 t. allspice, ground
Garnish: whipped cream or cinnamon sticks

Pour hot coffee into 2 mugs or heat-proof glasses. To each cup, add half of the heavy cream, brown sugar, vanilla and allspice. Mix until smooth. Garnish each serving with a dollop of whipped cream or a cinnamon stick. Serve immediately. Makes 2 servings.

Get everyone in your family together and leave a festive message on your answering machine! Be brave and sing, or take turns wishing a Happy Holiday season to your callers!

Aleathea Searles-Millard, Houston, TX

Holiday Pistachio Pie

Calico Inn Bed & Breakfast
Sevierville, TN

Looks very festive!

1-1/2 c. flour
1/4 c. walnuts, chopped
1-1/2 sticks margarine or butter, softened
8-oz. pkg. cream cheese, softened
1 t. vanilla
1 c. powdered sugar
1 c. frozen whipped topping
2 3-oz. pkgs. instant pistachio pudding
3 c. cold milk

Prepare the first layer by mixing flour, walnuts and butter. Spread in a 13"x9" glass pan. Bake at 350 degrees for 20 to 30 minutes. To make the second layer, mix cream cheese, vanilla, powdered sugar and whipped topping. Beat well and spread over the first layer. Refrigerate one hour. For the third layer, mix instant pudding with milk. Mix until dissolved; spread over the second layer. Top with additional whipped topping and nuts, if desired.

Make a holiday stationery basket so it will be easy to spread cheer during the holidays! Fill a basket with your favorite writing paper, envelopes, notecards, stickers and stamps. Put a big red bow on the basket handle!

Nancy Molldrem, Eau Claire, WI

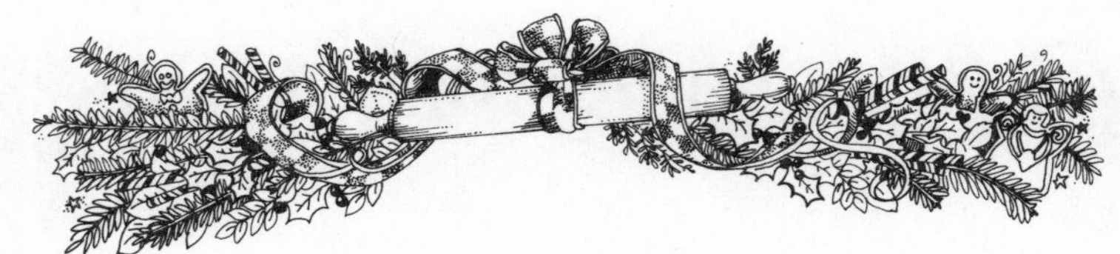

French Cream Mint Brownies

Phyllis Laughrey
Mount Vernon, OH

These bars freeze well.

1 c. sugar
1/2 c. butter, softened
4 eggs
16-oz. can chocolate syrup
1 c. flour
1/2 t. baking powder

Cream sugar and butter. Blend in eggs, chocolate syrup, flour and baking powder. Place crust in a greased, 15"x10"x1" jelly roll pan and bake at 350 degrees for 20 minutes. Chill in refrigerator while preparing filling.

Filling:

1/2 c. butter, softened
2 c. powdered sugar
2 T. milk
1 t. peppermint extract
2 to 3 drops green food coloring

Cream butter and powdered sugar together. Blend in milk, peppermint extract and food coloring. Spread evenly over crust. Refrigerate until firm. Prepare frosting.

Frosting:

1/2 c. butter
6 oz. semi-sweet chocolate chips

Melt butter and chocolate chips over low heat, stirring constantly. Pour evenly over filling. Chill slightly; cut into squares. Return to refrigerator and chill until firm.

Fill a bowl with whole nutmegs and a nutmeg grater. Guests will love fresh nutmeg in their coffee!

Delicious Custard Cake Pudding

Vintage Tea Room
Escondido, CA

Makes 20 servings...perfect for a dessert party!

1 lb. leftover tea bread or scones
2 oz. butter
2 tart apples, peeled and sliced
4 oz. dates, chopped or 4 oz. dried cranberries
8 whole eggs plus 4 yolks
2/3 c. sugar
1/2 t. salt
1/2 t. nutmeg
1/8 c. rum (or 2 T. rum extract)
1-1/2 qt. milk
1-1/4 c. heavy cream
powdered sugar
whipped cream
2 10-oz. pkgs. frozen raspberries or strawberries
2 T. corn starch
1/4 c. raspberry syrup

Crumble bread, or scones and spread in bottom of a baking dish. Dot with butter. Arrange sliced apples over the bread and add dates or cranberries to the top. To eggs add sugar, salt, nutmeg and rum. Beat until well combined. Combine milk and cream; heat to boiling, then scalding, watch for foaming. Carefully add hot milk to egg mixture and stir. Pour over contents in the baking dish. Add hot water to a roasting pan, place pudding dish in pan in one inch of water. Preheat oven to 375 degrees and bake for 45 minutes, or until knife inserted in center comes out dry. When done, remove dish and add powdered sugar and whipped cream to taste. Thaw and crush raspberries. Put corn starch in a bowl and add raspberry syrup. Heat in microwave, stirring the corn starch so there are no lumps. Add to thawed berries, heat until the sauce is slightly thickened. Top individual servings of pudding with approximately 2 tablespoons of raspberry sauce.

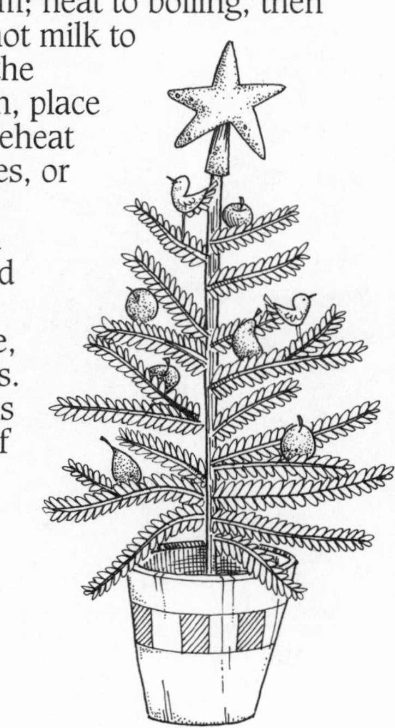

Christmas Snowflake Fudge

Helene Hamilton
Hickory, NC

Make this a very special tradition at your home.

6-oz. pkg. semi-sweet chocolate chips
1 T. shortening
1 c. pecans, chopped
12-oz. pkg. milk chocolate chips
14-oz. can sweetened condensed milk
1/2 c. flaked coconut

For first layer, melt chocolate chips with shortening in microwave or double boiler. Add nuts and spread in bottom of a buttered 8"x8" or 9"x9" pan. Cool while preparing second layer. Combine milk chocolate chips and sweetened condensed milk in a medium saucepan and cook over low heat, stirring frequently, until chips are completely melted and mixture is creamy. Pour over first layer and spread to cover. Sprinkle with coconut evenly and press gently. Cover and chill. Cut into small squares.

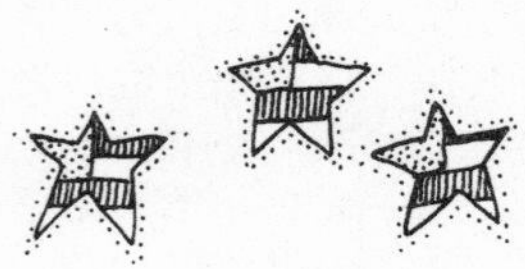

Offer different types of chocolate as coffee toppings...bittersweet, semi-sweet, milk and white chocolate. Set out a bowl of lemon zest, whole cardamom pods, whipped cream and a shaker of sugar for them to try also.

Coffee Bars

Jan Bree
Valley Center, CA

Reminiscent of a maple bar doughnut!

1/2 c. margarine or butter
2 c. brown sugar
2 eggs
1 c. liquid coffee
3 c. all-purpose flour
1/2 t. baking soda
1/2 t. salt
2 t. baking powder
1 t. cinnamon
1 c. walnuts, chopped
1 c. chocolate chips

Combine margarine, brown sugar and eggs, cream until blended. Pour in coffee. Add remaining ingredients, mix until blended. Pour into a greased cookie sheet at least one inch high, or large rectangular baking pan and bake at 350 degrees for 15 to 20 minutes until done.

Icing:

1-1/2 c. powdered sugar
2 T. margarine or butter, melted
3 t. maple syrup
milk to moisten

Prepare frosting by combining all ingredients until smooth. Frost bars while still warm.

Give your Christmas tree a toy theme...special toys or stuffed animals, secured with wire, will bring smiles and memories to your visitors!

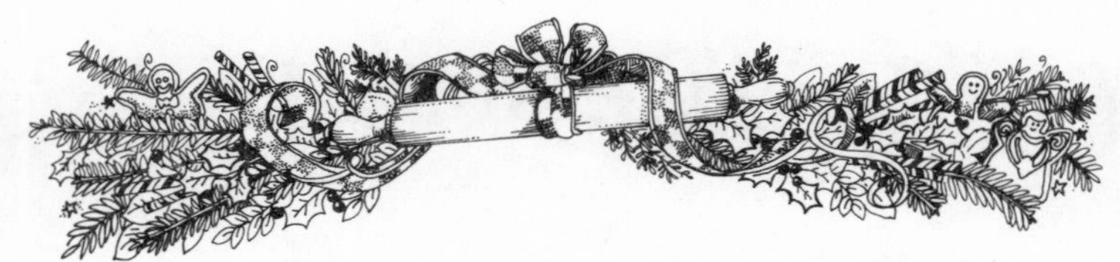

Italian Chocolate Cheese Pie

Grace Meletta
Carson City, NV

A special pie to prepare for the holidays.

1-1/2 lb. whole milk ricotta cheese
1/2 lb. sugar
1 lb. milk chocolate
2 T. vanilla extract
4 T. anise extract
6 eggs, beaten

In a large bowl, cream together cheese and sugar; blend well. Add chocolate to blender or food processor and finely chop. Add chocolate cheese to mixture; mix well. Add extracts and eggs; blend until creamy and smooth. Pour into 2, 8-inch pie shells. Bake at 375 degrees for one hour. Cool on rack for one hour, then refrigerate. Serve chilled.

Spray pinecones and nuts gold or bronze and place in a basket of fresh evergreens; a lovely centerpiece.

Kathy Grashoff, Ft. Wayne, IN

Black Bottom Pudding

Marty Darling
Coshocton, OH

You'll hope for leftovers!

1/4 t. salt
1 c. flour
1-1/4 c. sugar
2 t. baking powder
1/2 c. milk
2 T. butter
7 T. cocoa
1 egg
1/2 c. brown sugar
1-1/2 c. water, boiling
whipped cream

Sift together salt, flour, 3/4 cup of sugar and baking powder. Add milk, butter, 3 tablespoons of cocoa and egg. Mix together and pour into a greased, 8" square cake pan. Mix together remaining sugar, brown sugar and remaining cocoa. Sprinkle over mixture in cake pan. Carefully pour boiling water over all, do not stir. Bake at 375 degrees for 35 to 40 minutes. Cool, cut and serve upside down with whipped cream.

Make a beautiful fruit ice ring by adding 2 cups of crushed ice inside a 6-cup ring mold. Add your favorite fruits...grapes, cranberries, kiwifruit, orange slices or cherries. Pour 2 cups of cranberry juice over the fruit. Freeze overnight.

Holiday Hot Fudge Dessert

Kim Dubay
Freeport, ME

Serve with vanilla ice cream or whipped cream.

1 c. flour
2 t. baking powder
3/4 c. sugar
1/4 t. salt
6 T. powdered baking cocoa
1/2 cup nuts, chopped
1/2 c. milk
2 t. oil
1 t. vanilla
1 c. brown sugar
1-3/4 c. hot water

Mix flour, baking powder, sugar, salt, 2 tablespoons baking cocoa and chopped nuts. Add milk, oil and vanilla. Pour into a greased Bundt® pan. Combine brown sugar and remaining cocoa and sprinkle on top of mixture in pan. Pour hot water over entire batter. Do not stir. Bake at 350 degrees for 40 to 45 minutes. Serves 6 to 8.

A low centerpiece for your holiday table is very elegant. Red roses, baby's breath, ivy, white tulips and holly sprigs are perfect!

Mocha Truffles

Donna Nowicki
Stillwater, MN

So easy to prepare and the taste is unmatched!

24 oz. semi-sweet chocolate chips
8 oz. cream cheese, softened
3 T. instant coffee granules
2 t. water
1 lb. dark chocolate dipping chocolate

In a microwave-safe bowl, melt chocolate chips. Add cream cheese, coffee and water. Mix well with electric mixer. Chill until firm enough to shape. Shape into one-inch balls and place on a wax paper-lined cookie sheet. Chill for one to 2 hours, or until firm. Melt chocolate coating in a microwave-safe bowl. Dip balls in chocolate and place on wax paper to harden. Makes approximately 5-1/2 dozen candies.

As a guideline for your dessert party, choose 3 desserts for 8 people, adding another dessert for each additional 8 as your guest list grows.

Apple Jack

Mel Wolk
St. Peters, MO

An old-fashioned recipe that's a special treat.

1/4 c. shortening
2 c. sugar
1 egg
1 t. vanilla
2 c. flour
4 t. baking powder
1/2 t. salt
1 c. milk
2 or 3 large, tart apples
cinnamon

Cream together shortening and one cup sugar. Beat in egg and vanilla. Mix in flour, baking powder and salt. Add milk and beat until smooth. Slice apples about one-inch thick and layer in the bottom of a 13"x9" baking pan. Sprinkle with remaining sugar and cinnamon to taste. Spread cake batter over top. Bake in 350 degree oven for 40 to 55 minutes until cake is done and apples are cooked.

Make your guests feel really special! For your coffee and dessert party fill your table with seasonal fruits, nuts, and assorted cookies. Whip a quart of cream, sweeten with powdered sugar and flavor with vanilla. Spoon it into a chilled bowl and nest that bowl in a larger bowl filled with crushed ice. Arrange your desserts on a long dining or buffet table. Reserve one end or a separate table for a wonderful dessert fondue!

Christmas Date Pudding

Sally Davis
Payne, OH

Serve this special pudding for any occasion.

1 c. dates, chopped
3/4 c. water, boiling
1 c. sugar
1 egg, beaten
1 T. butter
1 t. baking powder
1 t. baking soda
salt to taste
1-1/2 c. flour
1/2 c. nuts
1 t. vanilla

Mix dates and water and allow to stand for 10 minutes. Don't drain water. Mix sugar, egg and butter, add to dates. Combine baking powder, soda, salt, flour and nuts and add to date mixture. Add vanilla. Pour into a greased and floured 13"x9" pan. Bake at 350 degrees for 35 to 45 minutes. Cool and serve with whipped cream.

A pretty napkin ring can be made by twisting a small screw eye into the end of a pinecone. Run a length of ribbon through the eye and tie around your napkin!

Kathy Grashoff, Ft. Wayne, IN

Christmas Apple Stack

Johny Cline
Collierville, TN

This family recipe is over 100 years old.

cookie dough
apples, cut into chunks
dried apples, cut into chunks
nuts, chopped
dash of vanilla
sugar

Plump dried apples by soaking them in apple cider or water for 30 minutes. Drain and set aside. Make your favorite cookie dough recipe and roll dough out to 1/4-inch thickness. Using a dinner plate as your guide, cut large circles in the dough. Bake according to your cookie recipe instructions. Alternately stack the cookie rounds with layers of apple chunks, chopped nuts, vanilla and sugar; as much as you'd like. Because this is a very old recipe the next step is a little different. The cake will now need to absorb the fruit and nuts. Place in a cake container and keep in the refrigerator for 3 weeks before serving.

Offer a variety of different flavors for your guests to try while they sip coffee. Place bowls of chocolate curls, orange rind, or cinnamon sticks on your table for guests to add to their individual cups of coffee.

Damson Custard Tarts

Jeannie Craig
Charlotte, NC

You can also substitute grape preserves in this recipe.

4 eggs, beaten slightly
1 c. sugar
1 c. damson preserves
pinch of salt
2/3 c. butter, melted
1 t. vanilla
16 tart shells, unbaked

Mix eggs and sugar, do not overmix. Add preserves, salt, butter, vanilla and blend. Turn into unbaked shells and bake at 350 degrees for 35 to 40 minutes or until set. Do not overfill the shells or the custard will fall when it comes out of the oven. Makes 16 tarts.

Loosely wind a strand of ivy garland around a grapevine wreath, secure with florist's wire. Wrap a strand of battery-operated tiny white lights around your garland, tuck the battery pack in the back out of sight. Intertwine gold and white ribbon around, tie in a large bow.

Mel Wolk, St. Peters, MO

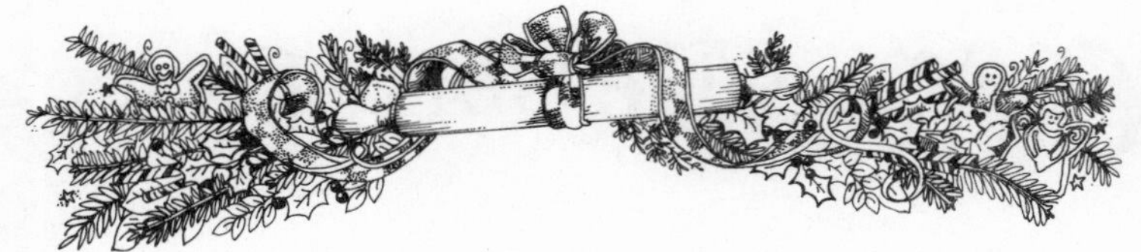

Caramel Apple Pie

Phyllis Laughrey
Mount Vernon, OH

Serve warm with cinnamon ice cream!

5 c. apples, peeled & sliced
1/2 c. sugar
1/4 c. flour
1-1/2 t. lemon juice
1/8 t. salt
1 t. cinnamon
8" unbaked pie shell

Combine all ingredients together and place in pie shell. Bake at 375 degrees for 20 to 25 minutes. Remove from oven and sprinkle with topping.

Topping:

6-oz. pkg. butterscotch chips
1/4 c. butter
3/4 c. flour

Melt together butterscotch chips and butter in a small saucepan over low heat. Allow to cool slightly, add flour. Mix together and sprinkle over pie. Return to oven and bake for an additional 25 minutes.

Top your coffee with spicy whipped cream. Whip 1/2 cup whipping cream with 2 tablespoons powdered sugar and 1/4 teaspoon ground cinnamon, add a dash of nutmeg!

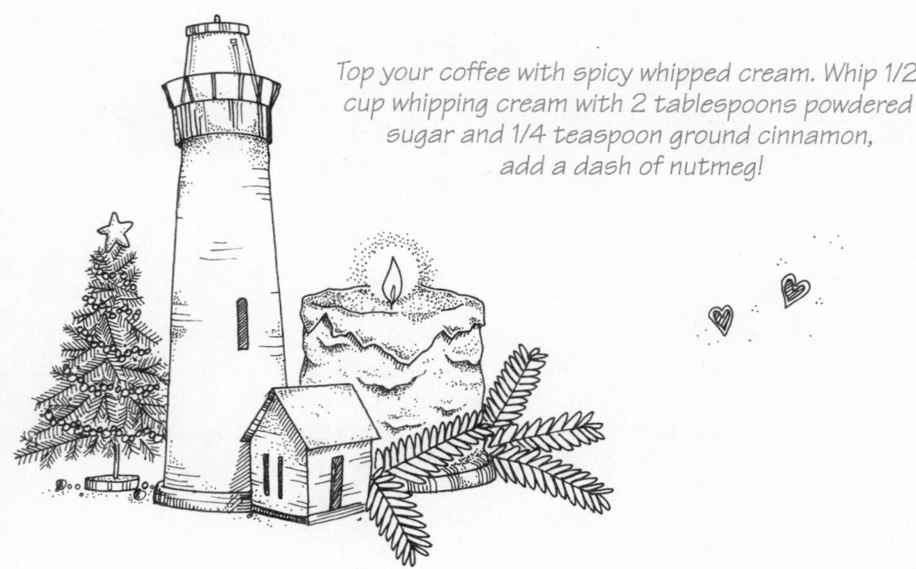

Oatmeal-Raisin Pie

Liz Kenneweg
Gooseberry Patch

Cook until the middle is soft when lightly touched.

3 eggs
1 c. light corn syrup
1/2 c. brown sugar
3 T. butter, melted
3/4 c. quick-cooking oats
1 T. all-purpose flour
1 t. cinnamon
1/4 t. salt
3/4 c. raisins
6-oz. ready-made graham cracker crust

Beat eggs together. Add corn syrup, sugar and butter beating on medium speed until thoroughly blended. Add remaining ingredients and mix. Pour into pie crust. Bake at 325 for 45 to 50 minutes or until top is golden and filling is just set in the center.

Prepare for a winter's snowstorm...stock your pantry with cocoa and mini marshmallows, keep some whipped cream and chocolate shavings on hand for a yummy cup of hot chocolate!

Chicken Scampi

Terri Dillingham
Windsor, NY

Try adding fresh broccoli and mushrooms for variety.

4 to 6 cloves garlic
2 T. parsley
1/8 c. lemon juice
1/4 c. white wine
1/2 c. olive oil
1/2 t. salt
1 t. garlic powder
2 T. oregano
1/4 c. chili sauce
2 boneless chicken breasts, cut into small pieces
Romano cheese, grated

Combine all ingredients. Bake at 450 degrees for 15 to 20 minutes. Serve over angel hair pasta with grated Romano cheese. Serves 2 to 3 people.

Don't wait until the last minute to shop! Keep catalogs close at hand and look through them year 'round keeping family and friends in mind. By the time Christmas comes you'll have all your presents without any last-minute shopping stress! You can truly enjoy the spirit of Christmas.

Quimby Cornish Pasties

Terry Waldron
Anaheim Hills, CA

Many years ago, Cornish coal miners would find these, along with tea, in their lunch pails.

1 c. shortening
4 c. flour
5 T. ice water
salt to taste
1 lb. steak, cubed into one-inch pieces
1 lb. lean pork, cubed into one-inch pieces
4 med. potatoes, cubed
1 lg. onion, diced
1 stick butter
salt and pepper to taste

Prepare dough by cutting shortening into flour. Add water and salt; form into a ball and refrigerate one hour. Remove dough from refrigerator and divide into golf ball-sized pieces. Roll one piece out on floured board until 8 or 9 inches in diameter. Repeat with remaining dough until you have made 7 or 8 pasties. On the bottom half of each dough circle place equal portions of steak, pork and potatoes. Add diced onion, a pat of butter, salt and pepper. Fold the top half of dough over the filling, dampen the edge with water, and crimp edges with a fork. Cut 3 slashes in the top to vent. Repeat with remaining dough circles. Lay pasties on an ungreased cookie sheet and bake at 400 degrees for 15 minutes. Brush with equal amounts of melted butter and water, reduce heat to 350 degrees and bake 15 minutes longer.

Decorate with mismatched mittens by slipping them over bottles and setting on your mantel.

Baked Ham & Apples

Susan Kennedy
Gooseberry Patch

Terrific served with sweet potatoes and steamed broccoli.

2-lb. fully cooked ham
3 apples
3/4 c. currant jelly
1/2 t. cloves, ground

Cut ham crosswise into 3/8-inch thick slices without cutting all the way through. Place in baking pan. Pare, halve and core one apple. Cut into thin slices. Arrange between ham slices. Halve and core the other 2 apples, without paring. Cut into wedges. Arrange apple slices around ham. Melt jelly in small saucepan over very low heat. Add ground cloves. Brush jelly glaze over ham. Bake at 350 degrees for 30 minutes or until heated through and glazed. Baste after first 10 minutes. Serves 4 with leftovers.

Tiny baby mittens that have been packed away can be displayed for Christmas! Lightly stuff each mitten with fiber-fill and sew the top closed. A ribbon loop at the top will make it easy to hang your precious ornament!

Mel Wolk, St. Peters, MO

Zoar Loaf

The Inn at Cowger House
Zoar, OH

The tangy dip is perfect served on the side!

2-1/2 lbs. ground chuck
2 eggs, beaten
2 lg. Granny Smith apples, peeled and chopped
1 sm. onion, chopped
1 c. cracker or dry bread crumbs
1/4 c. plus 4 T. molasses, divided
3 T. milk
4 T. catsup
2 t. mustard

Combine first 5 ingredients together and 1/4 cup of molasses and milk, mixing well. Place in a loaf pan and bake for 1-1/2 to 2 hours. In a small mixing bowl, combine catsup, remaining molasses and mustard together and pour over meat loaf. Bake 10 minutes longer.

Zoar Dip:

1 or 2 lg. Granny Smith apples, peeled and chopped
1 c. sour cream
1-1/2 T. horseradish

Mix ingredients together and refrigerate until ready to serve with meat loaf.

Yuletime Pasta Salad

Smith Runyan
Delaware, OH

A light, colorful salad.

2 c. bowtie pasta, cooked
6-oz. can white tuna, drained
1 c. mayonnaise-style salad dressing
1 c. broccoli flowerets
1 c. carrots, chopped
1 c. celery, sliced
1/2 c. sweet red pepper, chopped
1 T. dill weed
1/2 t. pepper

Combine all ingredients well; refrigerate overnight. Serves 6 to 8.

Attract all kinds of birds to your snowman! Before adding his hat, sprinkle the brim with wild-bird seed! Dried apples and raisins make fun eyes and a mouth, hollow out orange halves for his buttons!

Holiday Sweet Potatoes

Cindy Watson
Gooseberry Patch

Save your cored-out potatoes, mash and serve with leftovers!

20-oz. can sweet potatoes
16-oz. pkg. fresh cranberries
2 med. apples, peeled and chopped
1/2 c. water
1 c. sugar
1 c. walnuts, chopped
1 c. brown sugar
1 T. butter
1 stick butter

Drain sweet potatoes and lay on wax paper. Scoop out centers of potatoes; set aside. Combine cranberries, apples and 1/4 cup of water together in a saucepan, adding sugar to taste. Cook over medium heat for 10 to 15 minutes, or until cranberries burst. Add walnuts and stir well. Fill the center of each sweet potato with cranberry mixture and place in a baking dish. Combine brown sugar and butter in a small saucepan. Add remaining water slowly to create a syrup. Cook over medium heat until thick. Drizzle over potatoes and pat with butter. Bake at 325 degrees for 15 to 20 minutes just until heated through; don't over bake.

"I will honor Christmas in my heart, and try to keep it all year long."

-Charles Dickens, A Christmas Carol

Cottage Potato Casserole

Diana Claydon
Morgantown, WV

An adaptation on an old family favorite recipe created by Diana and her sister.

1/2 c. butter
1/2 c. milk
3 lg. potatoes, cooked, peeled, diced
1-1/2 c. ham, diced
1 c. colby cheese, shredded
2 T. parsley, chopped
1/2 slice fresh bread, torn
pinch of salt
pepper
1/2 c. corn flake cereal

Melt butter, add milk. Combine milk mixture with potatoes and next 6 ingredients. Top with cereal. Bake uncovered at 400 degrees for 30 minutes. Serves 4 to 6.

Be creative when decorating your holiday mantel! Cobalt blue vases and pitchers look beautiful combined with greenery, white poinsettias and tiny white lights. A forest of miniature evergreens look terrific beside a handmade cabin, and a gardener's mantel would include topiaries paired with forced bulbs, candles in terra cotta pots and children's gardening tools.

Holiday Potato-Cheese Soup

Dick & Marjie Alpers
Gahanna, OH

Wonderful when the weather turns cold!

2 c. potatoes, peeled and cubed
3 T. butter
1 sm. onion, chopped
3 T. flour
salt and pepper to taste
3 c. milk
1 c. Cheddar cheese, shredded
4 slices bacon, cooked crisp and crumbled

Cook potatoes until tender. Drain, reserving one cup water. Set potatoes and water aside. Melt butter in a saucepan over medium heat. Add onion and stir until tender, but not brown. Add flour, salt and pepper to onion, cook 3 to 4 minutes. Gradually add potatoes, reserved water and milk to onion mixture. Blend in cheese and bacon. Simmer on low heat for 30 minutes, stirring frequently.

Decorate an heirloom Christmas tree for your guest room. I decorate mine with linen handkerchiefs that belonged to my grandmother, pretty porcelain tea cups, beaded bags, lace fans and vintage Christmas postcards and calling cards from the early 1900's.

Linda Thompson, Mt. Juliet, TN

Italian Tortellini Soup

Teresa Sullivan
Gooseberry Patch

You'll get requests for this recipe!

1-lb. mild Italian sausage, casing removed
1 c. onion, chopped
2 lg. cloves garlic, chopped
6 c. beef stock
16-oz. can tomatoes, drained and chopped
8 oz. tomato sauce
1 lg. zucchini, sliced
1 lg. carrot, sliced
1 med. green pepper, diced
1/2 c. dry red wine
1 t. basil
2 t. oregano
8 oz. cheese tortellini
Parmesan cheese

Brown sausage and remove from skillet. Drain drippings. Add onion and garlic. Sauté 5 minutes. Combine meat, onion and garlic, beef stock, tomatoes, tomato sauce, zucchini, carrot, green pepper, wine and spices in a large pot. Simmer about 90 minutes until vegetables are tender. Add tortellini. Cook until tender. Serve with cheese.

"To all, to each, a fair good night, and pleasing dreams; and slumbers light."

-Sir Walter Scott

Mary's Homemade Bread

Debbie Musick
Yukon, OK

At age 84, Debbie's mother still bakes daily…giving bread to friends and family.

8 c. unbleached flour
2 T. yeast
4 c. warm water
1/2 c. sugar
1/3 c. solid shortening
1 t. salt

Mix flour and yeast, set aside. Combine water, sugar, shortening and salt. Stir to soften and melt shortening. Add flour mixture to liquid mixture. Using a large mixer, beat for 5 to 10 minutes. Let rise to double in size, about one hour. Knead and place in well greased pans. Let rise again to double. Bake at 350 degrees for 30 to 40 minutes.

Don't forget the upstairs of your home…decorate bathrooms, bedrooms and guest rooms, too!

Angel Food Trifle

Walnut Hill Bed & Breakfast
Avondale, PA

You can substitute a variety of different fruit if you'd like.

16-oz. pkg. angel food cake mix
1/3 c. sugar
1/4 c. cornstarch
1/4 t. salt
2 c. skim milk
1/4 c. egg substitute
1 t. grated lemon rind
1/4 c. lemon juice
2 8-oz. cartons vanilla low-fat yogurt
3 c. sliced strawberries
3 or 4 kiwis, sliced
6 strawberries, sliced

Prepare cake according to directions. Bake and cut into bite-sized cubes. Combine sugar, cornstarch and salt in saucepan. Gradually, add milk, stirring well. Cook over medium heat until mixture begins to thicken, stirring constantly. Remove from heat. Using a whisk, gradually add egg substitute, stirring constantly. Cook over medium heat about 2 minutes, stirring constantly. Remove from heat and cool slightly. Stir in lemon rind and lemon juice. Chill. Fold yogurt into cream mixture. Set aside. Place 1/3 of cake in bottom of 15-cup trifle bowl. Spoon 1/3 of custard over cake. Arrange half each of strawberry slices and kiwi slices around lower edge of bowl and over custard. Repeat procedure with remaining ingredients, ending with strawberry fans on top. Cover and chill 3 to 4 hours. Serves 15.

Tie a pretty bow on the handle of all your punch bowl mugs!

Christmas Plum Pudding

Joyce Milstead
Dallastown, PA

Prepare two weeks before Christmas Day.

1/2 c. dates, chopped
1/2 c. golden raisins
1/2 c. brandy

Soak together the above ingredients the night before making pudding.

2 c. flour
1 t. baking soda
1 t. cinnamon
1/2 t. nutmeg
1/2 t. salt
1 c. butter, softened
1 c. dark brown sugar
1/2 c. molasses
3 eggs
1/4 c. milk
1/4 c. brandy
1 c. almonds, slivered
2/3 c. coconut, flaked
1 c. plain bread crumbs

Combine and sift together first 5 ingredients. Cream butter and sugar well. Add molasses and eggs, beat in flour mixture and milk alternately. Add brandy. Stir in dates, raisins, almonds, coconut and bread crumbs. Pour into a greased 6-cup mold. Cover with buttered wax paper, tie with string and cover again with foil. Place on rack in large pot. Add water to just below rack. Cover and steam for 3 hours. Keep adding water to pan so it does not go dry. Cool and store at room temperature until Christmas Day. To serve, steam 2 hours, remove and cool 10 minutes. Loosen edges and invert onto plate. Decorate with holly and serve with brandy butter.

Brandy Butter:

1 c. powdered sugar
1/2 c. butter, softened
1 T. brandy
1 T. rum

Beat sugar and butter. Beat in brandy and rum and chill.

Hot Chocolate Eggnog

Debbie Parker
Gooseberry Patch

Enjoy a mug of this warm eggnog on a frosty evening!

1 egg
3/4 c. milk
1/2 c. water
3 T. unsweetened cocoa powder
1/2 t. nutmeg
2 T. sugar

Combine egg, milk, water, cocoa, nutmeg and sugar in electric blender or food processor and blend until well mixed. Transfer mixture to top of a double boiler. Heat, stirring occasionally, until mixture is steaming. Do not boil. Serve immediately. Serves one.

Little votive candles and silver ribbons intertwined among the baskets and bowls of your buffet table add sparkle.

HANDMADE
Christmas
JOY
HO HO HO

Michelle Corder
Alvaton, KY

A few years ago my husband's grandmother gave our family hand-knitted stockings. Although we didn't have a fireplace to hang them on, I bought an old mantel to decorate! After lots of scraping and a couple of coats of paint, it was ready! On our new mantel I placed a garland with white lights, red pillar candles in hurricane lamps, my snowman collection and, of course, our stockings. It was very pretty and so much fun for our sons to find their stockings on the mantel Christmas morning!

Carol Bull
Gooseberry Patch

Fragrant beeswax ornaments are easily made with supplies purchased at a craft or hobby shop. Purchase a block of pure beeswax and chop into small pieces. Remove the label from a clean, empty soup can, and gently pinch the can to make a pouring spout. Put the can in a pan filled with about 2" of water, add beeswax pieces to can and gently simmer until wax has melted. Beeswax is flammable, so don't leave stove unattended. When wax has melted, carefully pour into candle or candy molds that have been lightly sprayed with non-stick spray. Add a ribbon or candlewick hanger to the beeswax before the ornaments harden. If you use candlewick, use the ones with the metal core for stability. Just bend it into a U-shape and slip into the warm wax. Let the ornaments harden completely, or set in the freezer for quicker results. When completely hard, ornaments will easily pop out.

Aneda Bryk
Fredericksburg, TX

A garland of mittens can be easily made by recycling old sweaters! Hung from old clothespins, the garlands look so festive! To make your "mittens", turn an old sweater inside out. Pin the ribbing of the sweater sleeve cuffs and bottom ribbing around the sweater waist (this will be the wrists of your new mittens), creating 2 layers that won't slip. Cut a mitten shape from a piece of paper and lay your pattern on the sweater, be sure to place the mitten pattern wrists on the ribbing hem. Using a permanent pen, trace around mitten shape. Cut out mitten, adding a seam allowance as you cut. Pin 2 shapes together and sew on pen line. Turn mitten inside out, hang up and enjoy!

Sheri Vanderzee
Midland Park, NJ

Here is a simple craft to share with fellow dog lovers! This doggie stocking is sure to make our friends feel special on Christmas morning! Begin by making a dog bone pattern on plain paper. Lay the pattern on the wrong side of your fabric and trace around the edges. Make 4 bone shapes. Place the right sides of 2 bones together and stitch around the edges, leaving one end open so you can turn it right side out. Clip the seams and press flat along stitching. Turn fabric right side out and hand stitch the opening closed. Repeat with remaining 2 shapes. When completed, stitch both bones together along the edge...remember to leave the top open! Press and turn the right side out. Cut 6, 12" lengths of ribbon and hand-sew each randomly on the front of the stocking. Use the ribbon to tie dog biscuits to the front of your stocking and tuck lots of goodies and toys inside.

Cari Baker
Wayland, NY

Make a beautiful edible topiary for your next holiday gathering! Add a few small stones or marbles into the bottom of a terra cotta pot to keep it from tipping, then cut a block of oasis large enough to fill the pot. Gently push a large peppermint stick into the middle of the oasis then place a 9" foam cone over all but 3" of the peppermint stick. Place toothpicks in gum drops and then push them into the cone until the cone is completely covered. Cover the oasis with some Spanish moss, tie a raffia bow at the base of the peppermint stick and you'll have a terrific tree-shaped topiary!

Sing a Christmas carol while you're in the shower!

Helen Henkel
Southington, CT

If you're in a pinch for gift bags in the wee hours of Christmas morning, use paper bags! Use a holiday stencil, kitchen sponge and acrylic paints to stencil a design onto the bags. When the paint is dry, speckle the bags with a contrasting color of paint. You'll need an old paintbrush or stencil brush dipped into a small amount of paint. Using a plastic butter knife, draw it across the bristles to speckle the paint onto the bags; let dry. To make handles, take 2 lengths of twisted craft paper and tape or hot glue them to the bag.

Melissa Russo
Amsterdam, NY

Cookie cutter gift bags are so simple! You'll need your favorite cookie cutters such as a gingerbread man, Santa, or angels, brown paper lunch sacks, paint, markers, pencils, ribbon and glue. Position the cookie cutter in the center of your bag and trace the outline with a pencil. Use paint to outline your cookie cutter and let dry. Carefully erase pencil lines. Use markers to decorate your gingerbread man with eyes and a mouth, a cotton swab dipped in blush is perfect to create rosy cheeks! Tuck in your gift then fold over the top of the bag. Using a hole punch, punch a hole approximately 1" in from the edges of the bag and slide a length of ribbon through the holes to seal the gift inside!

Kathy Grashoff
Ft. Wayne, IN

Float orange peel stars in your Christmas punch; these are easy! Cut oranges into quarters, remove pulp, flatten each rind section and press a small star-shaped cookie cutter through it. You can also let them dry and add to potpourri!

Bridget Cote
Lunenburg, MA

I have an old, tall, wooden window shutter that was purchased at a yard sale. I've painted it in a festive holiday color and at Christmastime we place it in a corner of our kitchen. When Christmas cards arrive, we place them in the slats of the shutter for display. The shutter is both useful and it gives the room a country feel!

Norma Longnecker
Lawrenceville, IL

I am lucky enough to have the sled my husband played on when he was a child. All of his older brothers also played with it and the oldest brother is 89 years old! At Christmas I stand the sled by the front door and tie a spray of greenery with a red bow to the front of the sled and then hang a pair of antique skates.

Elizabeth Crum
Pittsburgh, PA

Being a flea-market and antique store fanatic, I am always on the lookout for clever vintage "finds" for my many collections. Recently I came across several antique Christmas books. This Christmas I plan to display my collection on my mantel along with old-fashioned Santas, garland and greenery. They would also make a terrific display in a hunter green wicker basket set on the hearth.

Go ice skating!

Pamela Erondy
Duanesburg, NY

I live on a rural route which makes mail delivery difficult on snowy, winter days. On those days, I leave a treat for my mail ladies...homemade biscuits or muffins with jam. At Christmas I fill a tin with homemade fudge, candy and cookies. Each one is topped with an ornament. It's my way of saying thanks for delivering all those packages!

Glenette Schantz
Rocky, OK

Painted jar candle holders are perfect for a holiday open house. Use them to light the steps to your door, set them on your mantel or along your buffet table. You can even send them home with your guests as a special favor. To make your candle holders, wash and dry small mouthed glass jars. Apply a coat of your favorite color, let dry. Spray with clear acrylic spray sealer, let dry completely and repeat with a second coat of sealer. Cookie cutters make excellent patterns for sponges; just cut around the edges with a pair of scissors. Snowmen, stars, moons, Christmas trees, stockings or mittens would all be pretty! When you've cut your desired shapes, dip sponges in water, then squeeze out excess. Dip sponges into paint and apply to your jar, let dry. Spray the entire jar with sealer. When sealer has dried, wrap an 18" strip of fabric around the neck of the jar and tie in a knot or bow. Place a tealight inside the jar, enjoy!

Greet visitors to your home with old-fashioned joys of the holiday season...the scent of balsam and fir, flowering narcissus bulbs, flickering candles, homemade cookies, strings of popcorn and tiny gingerbread men.

Marie Alana Gardner
North Tonawanda, NY

A holiday serving tray for any season! Remove the glass and cardboard backing from an 10"x8" or larger picture frame with wooden edges. Drill holes on the shortest sides of the wooden frame and attach a pull-style handle to each side. Cut a length of holiday fabric a little larger than your picture frame and glue it to the cardboard backing. Replace the glass in the frame then slip the fabric-covered cardboard behind the glass. You may want to attach felt or cork squares to the bottom of the frame to keep it from scratching any surfaces you set it on. You can change the fabric for any season or occasion!

Candy Hannigan
Monument, CO

I love using simple things when decorating for Christmas. A center-piece for a holiday luncheon might consist of several jars in different heights filled with peppermints, or an old bowl full of cranberries with a string of cranberries spilling out over the edge. I also might tie each guest's napkin around a new candy cane for them to use as a garnish in a cup of cocoa. Cookie cutters with handles also make great napkin rings. Cookie cutters also make terrific favors for guests to take home. Attach them to a small kitchen Christmas tree and they can take one as they leave!

Invite someone who lives alone to dinner this week.

Teresa Niell
The Colony, TX

For a homespun Christmas topiary, securely glue a styrofoam cone into a mini terra cotta pot. Cover the cone with glue and attach sheet moss. Next begin adding your ornaments! I glue on wooden gingerbread men, but you can also make some out of cinnamon dough with a cookie cutter if you prefer. Add some cinnamon stars; I cut mine out of modeling clay using mini cookie cutters and baked them according to package directions. When they're cool, spray them with adhesive and toss in a plastic zipping bag filled with cinnamon. Remove stars from the bag, dust off excess cinnamon and hot glue them on the cone. Add some pepper berries, baby's breath and tiny pinecones. Top off your tree with a yellow moon! I made mine out of clay I had cut with a mini cookie cutter and painted yellow. Swirl a few thin strands of raffia around the finished tree and glue a homespun bow around the rim of the pot.

Mary Mullen
Colleyville, TX

Pretty gift wrap can be made quickly and easily! Place freezer wrap, shiny side up, on a flat surface. Lightly scrape a knife over a crayon allowing the shavings to fall randomly on the paper. Place your favorite cookie cutter on the paper and lightly shave a crayon into the cutter opening. Move cutter to different areas on the freezer wrap and repeat as many times as you'd like. Place a piece of white tissue paper over the crayon shavings then cover the tissue paper with a sheet of brown kraft paper or a brown paper bag. Set your iron at a low temperature setting and iron over the brown paper bag until the crayon shavings melt. Gently remove the brown paper bag and you have lovely gift wrap!

Kim Smith
Brecksville, OH

This year make pretty holiday dining chair wreaths! Leaving a one-inch space at the top of the wreath for a ribbon, place 2 holiday floral picks on each side at the top of a 10" grapevine wreath. Gently bend the flowers and berries on the pick to fit the curve of the wreath. Loop a one-yard length of 1-1/2" ribbon around the wreath and between the floral picks. Tie in a bow over the back of your dining room chairs. An artificial evergreen wreath also looks charming tied with a plaid ribbon!

Christmas confetti plates add an elegant and very festive touch to any holiday occasion! Sprinkle any shape of holiday confetti…stars, snowflakes, or Christmas trees, over a clear, glass dinner plate. Place a second clear, glass plate of the same size on top to secure the confetti and to place food on. You could also use fresh herb sprigs, old-fashioned paper snowflakes or children's art.

Karen Hammen
Loveland, CO

An easy decorating idea that I use each year for our daughters' rooms and throughout the house are ivy topiary Christmas trees. We buy plugs of ivy from the local nursery, wire Christmas tree shaped topiary forms in different sizes and clay pots. After filling the clay pot with soil, we place the ivy plugs and wire forms in. We then wrap the ivy around the forms. Don't worry if your tree looks a little bare, decorating it will help and in a few years it fills in wonderfully!

Try to catch snowflakes on your tongue!

Pat Fessel
Haines, OR

This is a Yugoslavian tradition that we learned while we were in Seattle. On St. Nicholas Day, December 6, place 1/4 cup of whole wheat berries in a shallow dish and sprinkle with water. Each day afterward, sprinkle lightly with water to encourage germination, a spray bottle is perfect for this. Let the sprouts continue to grow until Christmas Eve when they should reach their full height of 6 inches. Place a pillar or votive candle in the center and light. The new growth of wheat symbolizes prosperity, health and happiness for the coming year. You can even deliver a bag of wheat berries tied with a red ribbon along with the traditional story and directions to friends just before St. Nicholas Day.

Belinda Gibson
Amarillo, TX

Decorate a small Christmas tree in your dining room or kitchen with teacups! Tie ribbons on the handles of the teacups and then tie the ribbons on your tree branches...add white lights and drape lace over the branches; beautiful!

Melissa Ing
Glastonbury, CT

I have some beautiful old evening bags that have been handed down to me from family and friends. To be able to display and enjoy them at Christmas, in each I place a Teddy bear or two, add vintage silk flowers, a Victorian postcard or antique baby photo, old ornaments or jewelry. If the purse has a handle, it makes a nice door decoration.

Ruth Palmer
Glendale, UT

I like to start early in my Christmas celebration and often prepare "countdowns" for those that I love. One year I bought Christmas coloring books for my grandchildren. I wrote numbers from 1 to 25 on the pages with instructions to color one page each day from December 1st until Christmas. On the Christmas page I wrote Merry Christmas and decorated it with stars and stickers. For the adults on my list I copied 24 Christmas poems, thoughts and inspirational sayings on separate slips of paper. These were folded and put inside a jar. Directions were glued to the outside of the jar in the form of a label telling the recipient to read one thought per day until Christmas.

Kathy Grashoff
Fort Wayne, IN

This is a very easy gift for Christmas! You'll need a lunch-size brown paper bag, a length of 2" to 3" wide fabric, torn homespun looks terrific, and a small artificial or live Christmas tree. Place the tree in your bag and fold the bag down on the inside until you have a height you like. Wrap the fabric strip around the bag and gently cinch it around the plant. Tie a simple bow or knot. It's a simple but beautiful gift to give. Don't forget to water the tree if it's real!

"Use what talents you possess: the woods would be very silent if no birds sang there except for those that sang best."

-Henry Van Dyke

Sally Kelly
Akron, OH

On Thanksgiving I like to put out a special treat for our neighborhood birds. I must admit, the squirrels like this as well! Make two slits in the bottom of a clean, empty yogurt carton. Thread a piece of yarn or string through the slits and knot, leaving a loop long enough to hang the container over a small tree branch. Spread peanut butter on the outside and bottom of the carton, then roll in birdseed. Hang from a nearby tree branch. You'll love watching the birds as they enjoy this treat!

Ann Aulwes
Waterloo, IA

Decorate an outside tree for your fine-feathered friends! Begin by cutting your slices of stale bread with festive cookie cutters. Use a straw to make a hole in the top of each slice. In a small bowl combine peanut butter and a small amount of vegetable oil. Spread the mixture on the top and sides of your bread. Press sunflower seeds onto the edges of your shape and sprinkle birdseed onto the center. Press lightly so the seeds will stick well. Thread a piece of raffia through the hole so you can hang it outside. You can also cut oranges in half and hollow them out, fill them with dried cranberries and set among the tree branches. Just sit back and watch your backyard friends enjoy their holiday treats!

Tuck chunky votives in a wooden bowl then surround them with dried artichokes, green apples and rose hips for a natural centerpiece.

Gaye Leighley
Cedar Crest, NM

A "Family Tree" is so easy to make! We have great grandparents, grandparents, children, aunts, uncles and cousins in our tree! The children take particular delight in looking for their leaf prints. To make a Family Tree simply trace around everyone's hands on various shades of green felt. Cut out the handprints and ask each person to sign and date theirs. When you have enough to make a tree, simply tape them to a door in a tree shape. The trunk can be constructed out of brown felt. Storage is also easy as you just take the tape off and store with all your other Christmas decorations.

Patricia Pascale
No. Providence, RI

Each year at Christmas I trace my children's hands. I use red construction paper for my son and green for my daughter. I trace their hands and attach them to the handprints from previous years; making a garland of their tiny, little hands. I write the year on the back and hang them by alternating colors to see how much their hands have grown over the years. It brings back wonderful memories for our family when we hang them each year.

"The best way to cheer yourself up is to try to cheer somebody else up."

-Mark Twain

Donna Wheeler
Norwalk, IA

On a table in my entryway I loosely drape a 40-year old baby blanket and sit the stuffed toys from my adult children's childhood on it. I include a doll in a dress made by my mother and add old toys and alphabet blocks. This display is a favorite when the kids gather for Christmas at Mom's. Another decorating tip: if you pick up odd drinking glasses at garage and store sales, tuck votives or tea lights inside. Arrange your candle holders among greenery on your mantel, coffee table or buffet table; the more the merrier!

Maureen Baly
Sylvan Lake, IL

This year make a special Christmas treat for your dog; a dog collar scrunchie! Every month I make new scrunchie for my dog, Dave, to wear over her collar. Because each dog is a different size, measure your dog's collar width and double it and add 1/2". For example Dave's collar is 1-1/2" wide so I cut the fabric 3-1/2" wide by 45" long. Turn right sides together and sew a 1/4" seam allowance. Turn the scrunchie right side out and slide it over the collar cutting the length if necessary to get a good fit. A terrific gift for your favorite dog or dog lover on your gift list!

Debbie Byrne
Clinton, CT

These are the prettiest Christmas ornaments ever! Purchase clear glass ornaments that have a hook in the top that can be removed and replaced. Remove the hook and add a few drops of up to 3 colors of acrylic paint inside the ornament...white, red and green look great together! Swirl the paint carefully around the inside and allow the paint to dry. You can even decorate the outside of the ornament with glitter glue. These make wonderful and unique gifts.

Julie Dobson
Loma Linda, CA

Each year on the first Sunday of December I host a cookie exchange for my friends. In November I ask my guests to send the recipe for the cookies they'll be bringing so I can prepare a cookie exchange cookbook. We enjoy a sit-down luncheon of homemade soups, salads and breads and each guest brings 8 dozen of one type of Christmas cookie. Last year we composed the "rules" of the cookie exchange! You must arrive in holiday attire, your cookies must be unique and all the dads will be babysitting! Although they don't seem to mind considering 8 dozen cookies will be coming home with their wives! We finish the day with flavored coffees and teas while sampling some of the cookies we've gathered. As each guest leaves, she receives a copy of the cookie exchange cookbook which includes all recipes from that year and several recipes from the luncheon.

Compliment someone today!

Debbie Prellwitz
DeKalb, IL

I like to bring snowflakes inside to decorate our country Christmas tree. It does take a bit of advance planning, but is well worth it. Every year in late July or August I go out along the country roadsides and collect the flowers from Queen Anne's Lace. I look for all size blooms, making sure they are still white and haven't turned dark in the centers. I then come home and press these beautiful blooms between pieces of wax paper and place them between the pages of heavy books. There I leave them until December. Every year, the weekend after Thanksgiving, our family travels to a Christmas tree forest to select our holiday tree. After we find the perfect tree we take it back to the barn then warm up with hot cider or cocoa and freshly popped popcorn. After we get our "perfect" Christmas tree up in the family room, with a crackling fire and Christmas carols playing softly in the background, we discover our tree isn't so perfect after all. So, after all the lights and ornaments are on our tree, I take out my giant snowflakes and place them on the branches of our tree. They are fragile, so they have to be handled with care. I fill the tree with these lacy snowflakes…each one is unique. They add just the right touch to our Christmas tree, making it the perfect tree after all!

Joy Hamby
Cookeville, TN

If you get a late start, you don't have to press your Queen Anne's Lace flowers to have beautiful snowflakes! During December I will go to places I have seen Queen Anne's Lace growing during the summer months. By wintertime the blooms of these wildflowers have dried naturally to resemble a starburst. I cut them, leaving several inches of the main stem, and spray paint them white. I now have a lacy snowflake that I can use to decorate my Christmas tree, wreath, or packages.

Mel Wolk
St. Peters, MO

Snow saucers take no time to make and look like you've spent hours on them! They make wonderful gifts for teachers, neighbors, or special friends. Cookies for cookie exchanges and homemade candies look even more festive when given in a snow saucer! Begin by painting the bottom and sides of a clean 6" terra cotta saucer with acrylic paint in brick red. Let dry. Paint the inside and top edges of the saucer with acrylic paint in country blue or evergreen. Two coats may be needed to cover well. Tear a sponge into several small 1/2" pieces and dip into cream or white acrylic paint. On the inside of the saucer, dab three round shapes to make a snowman figure. Use a toothpick dipped in orange paint for the nose and brown paint for the twig arms. Don't forget to give your snowman eyes, a mouth and buttons. Dip another toothpick in cream or white and write "Let it Snow" at the top of the saucer over the snowman. You can even add a few snowflakes around the snowman. Let the saucer dry completely, then dip a dry toothbrush in the cream or white paint and spatter the inside of the saucer. Let dry and then spatter the bottom and sides also. When the paint is completely dry, spray the saucer with two coats of clear polyurethane. Your saucer will be very durable, and may be gently washed by hand.

"That man is richest whose pleasures are cheapest."

-Henry David Thoreau

Wendy Lee Paffenroth
Pine Island, NY

The Heart & Soul Hot Pack is great in the winter for warming up children who come in from ice skating or playing in the snow, as well as warming up a cold bed or soothing stiff, sore joints! Begin by cutting 2, 14" squares of cotton material and 2, 14" squares of cotton batting. Place each piece of batting on the wrong side of each square of fabric and quilt the batting to the cotton with a sewing machine. Place the right sides of each fabric square together and pin around the edges. Stitch edges closed remembering to leave an opening on one side. Turn the bag right side out and carefully pour 2 bags of barley in the opening. You can substitute one bag of whole grain rice (not minute rice) or substitute dried lentils for one bag of barley if you'd like. I buy a large bag of gingerbread potpourri and combine it with 10 bags of barley. This is enough for 5 hot packs and gives the bags a nice scent. Don't use vanilla extract however; it burns when heated. Pin the opening of your bag closed and slip stitch over it to keep the barley securely inside. When you need to warm up frosty toes, just slip your hot pack into the microwave and heat for 2 to 3 minutes. Watch carefully and check often; the hot packs will steam if you leave them in too long. A pack will last about 6 months depending on how often you use it. Just leave it in your linen closet and heat it up when you need to be toasty warm! It's called the Heart & Soul Hot Pack because on a cold winter's night it warms you to your soul.

For a stunning centerpiece, place a potted poinsettia in a crystal punch bowl, and add a strand of white lights inside the bowl. You can even leave it up after the holidays are over… a bright, sparkling addition to winter.

Mary Rose Kulczak, Temperance, MI

Holiday Memories

Linda D'Amico-Romano
Canonsburg, PA

It was a cold November day in 1969 when my grandfather, Nono, was watching me while my mother and grandmother, Nani, went shopping. As it was getting close to Christmas, Nono and I started talking about what we would like. He told me that he would like a wristwatch and I told him that all I wanted was a rocking chair that played music. Now, I had never seen a rocking chair that played music, but I guess in all my five-year old wisdom, I figured there had to be one out there somewhere. Time passed and before I knew it, Christmas Eve was upon us. The whole family gathered at Nani and Nono's house for the traditional Italian Christmas Eve dinner. After dinner was over, the kitchen cleaned, it was time to open gifts from aunts, uncles and grandparents.

After the gifts were opened, one object remained covered in a blanket in the center of the room. At that point, Nani and Nono told me that it was mine. A hush fell over the room as the blanket was removed and there sitting in the middle of the room, was a rocking chair and when it rocked, it played Brahm's Lullaby! It was for me from my Nono. Years later my Mom told me that Nono hunted everywhere until he found the rocking chair that played music. The rocking chair proudly sits in its own special corner of my living room; a reminder of a special gift from a very special person.

"Remembrance, like a candle, burns brightest at Christmas-time."
-Charles Dickens

Holiday Memories

Kathy Turcotte
Browns Mills, NJ

I remember one Christmas when I was little, money was very tight that year, and my family had no money for a tree. Out front on our walkway, magically appeared one very perfect Christmas tree. We brought it in and Mom decorated it. The tree was done all in blue; blue satin balls, blue lights and angel hair on the finished tree. It was the most beautiful tree I had ever seen. In all the years that followed, we never did find out where that mysterious tree came from, but it made one Christmas very special in my memory.

Pat Habiger
Spearville, KS

Living on a farm growing up with two brothers, we always had chores with the chickens, pigs and cows. We also had great memories of lying in the haystack in the summer and soaking up the country sun, but my best memory is ice skating on our small farm pond. It was snowing lightly and I remember looking up toward the pasture as Dad pitched the hay out of the wagon and the cattle followed slowly behind. Our big red barn kept the cattle warm in the winter and to me it always had the feeling of the manger at Christmastime.

Pop a big bowl of popcorn, snuggle under a quilt and enjoy a classic Christmas movie with your family.

Belinda Gibson
Amarillo, TX

Growing up we always had Christmas stockings that were packed with candy, nuts, and fruit. My parents never wrapped presents because Santa always brought them on Christmas Eve and the entire living room would be filled. The day after Christmas, my mom got very sick and during the night my dad had to take her to the hospital. My dad woke me up to tell me where he was going and while he was gone, he asked me to pack a bag for Mom. As I hurried to pack the bag, I went through my mother's belongings and noticed that she had nothing new. All that she had was old and worn. I sat down and thought of all the wonderful new things we had just been given for Christmas. I knew then and I continued to be reminded throughout my life, that my mother always gave us everything she had. I learned the real meaning of the giving spirit of Christmas that year.

Marlene McGovern
Brunswick, ME

Early settlers of Massachusetts lit their Christmas candles from the stub of a candle remaining from the previous year's Christmas. This idea touched my heart and I decided from then on I would do the same thing. There is a continuum in all of our families...and we have celebrations with loved ones having left us and new members having been welcomed. It does not matter what our belief system is around the upcoming holidays, a candle saved from year to year to brighten the light at our table can somehow continue to bring us together in love and in thought.

Begin a tradition of taking your children to see The Nutcracker Suite.

Holiday Memories

Carolyn Gulley
Cumberland Gap, TN

We lived on a farm when I was growing up and when it snowed, we would play outside until we froze! We would then go inside, take off our wet clothes and hang them up to dry while Mom made some hot chocolate. The best times I remember were when Dad was home. Together he would build igloos and ride sleds with us, or rather, watch us, and haul us back up the hills on the tractor. I'll never forget the fun, or the frozen fingers!

One of my favorite Christmas memories is when family would come to our house to celebrate. My mom has eleven brothers and sisters and my dad has six brothers and sisters, so there was plenty of family around. The kids, of course, had fun playing together, but the adults were the real celebration. I can remember my mom and aunts poking pins down into the presents and shaking them to find out what was inside and then laughing until they cried! The fun, the food and the family fellowship...what memories of home!

Start a collection of Christmas books! Look for them at garage sales and secondhand book shops. Pile them in a big basket and let your children choose one to read before bedtime during the holidays.

Glenda Geoghagan
DeFuniak Springs, FL

In the late 1950s, when I was a young girl, my younger sister and two younger brothers awoke on Christmas morning excited at the prospect of what Santa had left us that year! As was the custom, we each had a designated area in the living room where Santa was to leave our presents. These spots were not labeled; however, we all knew that he would know, without a doubt, where to leave each child's bounty. After dressing and making our beds, as was our annual routine, we all rushed into my living room with a bang! How excited we were to find an assortment of dolls, games, nuts and candies. As I scurried to my corner of the living room, my eyes stopped on a pair of panty hose in a pile to the side. It was the best present that any girl could have ever dreamed of receiving! You see, I had not been allowed to wear these previously; although many of the other girls in my class at school had worn them for some time. I had hardly noticed anything else that lay in my small corner.

About that time, my parents came into the room, just in time to see me in my inexperienced manner, pulling the panty hose onto my feet. The laughter began with my mother and then became a contagious roar in the room. When the laughing died down, my mother explained to me that she had sat in that spot the night before and taken off her hosiery before retiring for the night. How embarrassed and disappointed I was to learn that Santa had not left this wonderful gift for me. I still look back on that early Christmas and remember, with mixed, emotions, how I felt. But fortunately, I can now laugh along with the rest of my family!

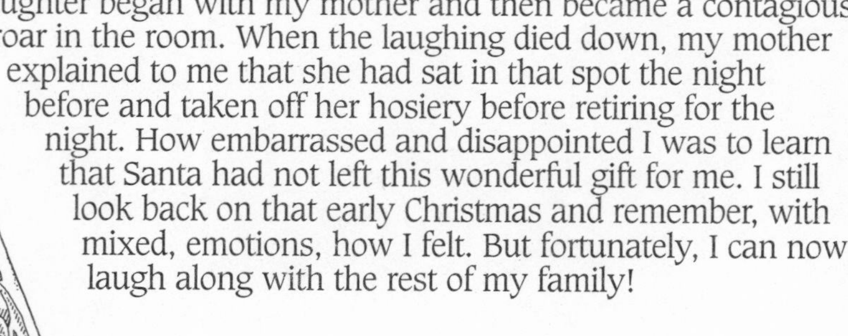

Gather your family together for some quiet time during the holidays. Play board games, read aloud, or have a picnic in front of the fireplace.

Holiday Memories

Caroline O'Brien
Vero Beach, FL

When I was approximately seven years old, in the 1930s, I received a navy blue sweater for Christmas that had my initials, CME, embroidered in red on the sleeve. I kept if for "good" which was seldom, since we didn't have an automobile and lived three miles from town. When I did want to wear it, I found I had almost outgrown it. How awful! I now have pillowcases embroidered with my husband's and my initials and I make myself use them, but think of my sweater with every glance.

Amy McGrew
Miamisburg, OH

Every Christmas Eve day my family and I go for a hayride on a wagon pulled by horses. We bundle up and take Christmas music along. As we are escorted through the snow, in the crisp fresh air, we sing Christmas carols and ring big jingle bells we wear around our wrists. It's fun for the grandparents, parents, children and grandchildren. After the hayride, we drive back to Grandma's house for hot chili and cornbread.

Kids still get pleasure from the simple things...a box of crayons, colorful marbles, a jigsaw puzzle, stuffed animals, Raggedy Ann or Andy, classic adventure books, or a train set. These never go out of style.

Rose Greene
Accord, NY

My fondest memories of my childhood are going with my grandmother and my Aunt Mae into the woods to gather creeping cedar and red holly berries to make Christmas wreaths. After gathering the creeping cedar, we would go home and have a cup of tea and a slice of home-made bread. We would then sit around the kitchen table and make the wreaths. I still remember how we made them.

Susan Hochworter
Niagara Falls, NY

It was two years ago Christmas day and we had everyone at our home for Christmas dinner. My dad hadn't been feeling well and I couldn't help thinking how he had aged and how frail he looked. After everyone left, I cried thinking this might be the last Christmas with my dad. The next day in the newspaper, there was a small cartoon and verse that I felt was addressed to me. It read, "Yesterday is the past. Tomorrow is the future. Today is a gift, that's why we call it the present." It immediately made me sorry that I had been depressed that Christmas Day. Why hadn't I just enjoyed that Christmas with my dad and family? My dad was not with us the next Christmas, but that small verse got me through a lot of bad days that year. I try very hard to repeat that verse to others and to live my life with it in mind. I believe that verse was there for me that day...appreciate each day and treat it as a gift.

Stencil Merry Christmas signs for all your pets! Add them to a dog house, fish tank, kitty bed or bird cage!

Nancy Molldrem
Eau Claire, WI

Holiday Memories

Ellen DeWitt
Delaware, OH

The year we got married, we lived in Grand Lake, Colorado. It started snowing Thanksgiving day and didn't stop until after New Years. By Christmas Eve the snow was already four feet deep. We dug a pathway out to the road, and all the dogs could do for outside exercise was to run up and down that path, they couldn't make it over the snow bank. As the sun set that evening, we discussed the fact that somehow we had overlooked getting a tree. My fearless husband said, "Never fear, my dear, I'll go get us a tree," and proceeded to dress himself in every layer of warm clothing he owned. We were renting a romantic A-frame in a lovely woods. On the wall were a pair of old snow shoes. My husband strapped them on and bravely stepped off the porch...and sank to his armpits in the snow. Imagine trying to move with snowshoes strapped to your feet, buried in four feet of snow! Tim floundered around the side of the house and disappeared into the darkness. Periodically, I heard him shouting (and cursing) and eventually he reappeared with a pine branch in his hand. "Merry Christmas," he told me. "I got to the back of the house and couldn't take another step. I pulled this off a tree." I put the branch in a tin can, filled it with stones, and hung one glass ball on it. We love to tell people about that first Christmas: the snow, snowshoes and our Christmas tree.

After a wintertime walk, wash your dog's paws with a washcloth dipped in lukewarm water. Salt and chemicals used to melt ice on sidewalks and roads can irritate their tender footpads.

Carol Wakefield
Indianapolis, IN

Every Christmas Eve after we return from Church services, my husband and I turn out every light in the house, and light all the candles...every wall sconce, kitchen candle, bathroom votive and candlestick on the mantel. We then gather the children by the Christmas tree to read The Night Before Christmas and the Christmas story from Luke. Then each child is escorted to bed and tucked in by candlelight. It is truly magical to walk through the house lit only by candlelight and go to bed under warm, handmade quilts. The children fall asleep almost immediately, anticipating Christmas morning.

Kris Bailey
Conklin, NY

Every child secretly dreams of catching a quick glimpse of Santa and his reindeer. One Christmas Eve memory I would like to share is when my sister and I thought we heard Santa and his furry team outside our bedroom. We were sooo excited! Our eyes grew big and our hearts skipped in our chests. We jumped out of bed to investigate for ourselves. Only to find Mom and Dad were at the top of the stairs waiting to greet us. Falling asleep that night was not easy! Years later the truth be known, what we really heard were my parents shaking a set of old sleigh bells. What makes this memory so special is that even though we now know it was Mom and Dad making all of the racket, that night, in our hearts, we truly believed in Christmas magic!

Set ice luminarias along your pathway as a magical way to welcome friends on a cold winter's night.

Holiday Memories

Becky Graver
Hays, KS

When my two sisters and I were little, our parents would put us aboard the train and send us to our grandparents for Christmas Eve. All our aunts, uncles and cousins would gather there where we would celebrate Christmas Eve together. We had lots of baked goodies and would put on skits to entertain the adults, play games and wait for the big moment when the door bell would ring and Santa would appear bearing gifts for all. What fun! We three girls would climb into the big, old four poster bed and snuggle together to dream of what was yet to come on Christmas Day. Our parents would arrive the next day with all our relatives and spend a festive and merry Christmas together. What special memories I have of those holiday times we shared at our grand-parents' house.

Mary Rose Kulczak
Temperance, MI

There is something magical about a nighttime winter's walk. One year, my sisters, mother and I bundled up the children and took them on a walk. It was a clear, star-filled night, and as we walked we pointed out the constellations to the children. They were thrilled to be able to walk in the dark and their cold cheeks didn't slow them down a bit. We talked and shared memories of the year, discussed our hopes, dreams and resolutions for the coming year. My nieces and nephews still remember that magical night when they were allowed to walk in the dark on a wintry eve.

Are you traveling with little ones this Christmas? Make it fun for all. Wrap bows and garlands around the luggage rack of your car, take plenty of activity books, snacks, fruit juice, pillows and blankets.

Joanne Wachter
Perry Hall, MD

For the past 21 years, I anxiously await midnight on Christmas Eve. At 11:55 PM, I get out of bed, put on my robe and slippers and go outside. As the clock strikes midnight, I look up into the sky and look at all the beautiful, twinkling stars and say a prayer. There is so much holiness and magic in the air at midnight that is the epitome of the Christmas holiday.

Nancy Machcinski
Erlanger, KY

When my brother and I were youngsters, we both looked forward to Christmas with much enthusiasm. My father would catch a bus to ride to town and pick out a tree, then he would have to walk home with it. The tree was decorated on Christmas Eve and my mother would decorate the house and put the gifts around the tree after we had gone to bed. My brother and I found it very hard to go to sleep and stay asleep. We would set the alarm for 5:00 AM and after we opened the gifts, my mother would fix a large breakfast. Relatives would drop by, off and on, until early afternoon. Then we would prepare to go to an aunt and uncle's house for supper. They didn't have any children, so we were a welcome addition to their Christmas. We had no car in the 1940's, so we had to catch two buses, but we gladly did it. It seems to me that there was, in those days, a feeling in the air that could almost be touched with joy and purity for the day.

Holiday Memories

Judy Kelly
St. Charles, MO

For as many years as I can remember, our family has eaten a traditional Slovak Christmas Eve dinner. The dinner begins with oplatky, Christmas wafers, served with a touch of honey. A variety of soups are served that always include sauerkraut and mushrooms. One of the side dishes served is bobalky which is tiny balls made of homemade bread dough served in a sweet poppyseed sauce. Another of the side dishes is cream of wheat made with sugar, cream, cinnamon and lots of melted butter. Fresh fruits are served, and my mother always presented this in a fruit salad. A dish of stewed prunes was always on the table, but was not one of the most requested dishes. Fish is an important part of the meal and our choice was always breaded deep-fried shrimp served with homemade seafood sauce. Rounding out the meal were my mom's wonderful homemade nut and poppyseed rolls and bread.

Over the years my sisters and I have learned to make most of the traditional foods. Now, when we can't all be together on Christmas Eve, we try to serve the meal we enjoyed so much when we were growing up. We are sharing it with our grandchildren and hopefully, creating wonderful holiday memories for them.

"The best portion of a good man's life,
his little, nameless, unremembered
acts of kindness and love."
-William Wordsworth

Pamela Ekern
Parker, CO

Teddy, dressed in a jaunty green and red plaid hat and vest, first entered our family as a gift to my grandmother in 1942. Each year, after feasting on prime rib and cheesy potatoes, Teddy becomes the guest of honor at the Christmas dinner table. But, before he makes his "toasts," each guest at the table is given a slip of paper on which to write a prediction, a bit of advice and a kind word for someone else at the dinner table. The paper is folded and the author's name written on the front. Then, it's Teddy's turn. Out of a drawstring pouch on which Grandmother lovingly embroidered "X-mas Tidings" and attached to Teddy's paw, comes last year's messages. They are distributed by the host or hostess and read by the person who wrote the words. If that person is not at the table this year, their message is read by the person for whom it was written.

As happens, there will be members of the family who are no longer with us, or who cannot come to Christmas dinner. However, through their wishes, advice and predictions, they still share Christmas with us. After the readings, the new tidings are put in a sealed envelope and entrusted to Teddy's care until next year. Teddy himself visits the home of the guest who will be hosting next year's Christmas dinner. A family mystery has always been how each year, Teddy removes from his sealed pouch, those words which may be too painful for someone at the table. I guess that's a secret between Grandmother and Teddy.

Holiday Memories

Ruth Palmer
Glendale, UT

Her name is Ann Kathleen and she and I have long since passed the half century mark. She'll be nestled in her wooden cradle underneath my Christmas tree this year, as she has been for many years past. At first glance, she looks quite respectable, but under the baby cap that she wears, a deep crack runs across her head and the painted hair is chipping off. A peek under her covers would reveal a dirty stuffed body. The simple voice box that once said "mama" is broken and silent. Traces of bright red nail polish remain on her fingers and toes where a little girl painted them many years ago. I was seven the year Santa left her for me. Times were simpler then. You could ask almost any little girl what she wanted for Christmas and the reply would be "a doll". Ask her what she wanted to be when she grew up and she'd reply "a mommy". It was no different for me as I played house and mothered my doll. I dreamed of the home and family I would someday have. Sometimes as I look at her, I realize that even a junk dealer would probably look at her in her torn and tattered condition and relegate her to the trash heap. She only has meaning for me. You see, she is a symbol of all I hold dear and a reminder that yes, dreams do come true. I grew up and became a teacher, but eventually realized my lifelong dream. I married my prince and became a "mommy"! And would you believe my two oldest daughters are named Ann and Kathleen.

Have a clothing and old toy round up with your family. Giving away "gently worn" and outgrown clothes and toys is a wonderful way to share the Christmas spirit.

Lori Stricklen
Blue Creek, WV

My grandmother didn't know what she could get me for a Christmas gift in 1992 and she questioned my mother, who suggested that Granny write down some of the memories of Christmases of her childhood. She wrote a story, calling it "I Remember Christmas". Granny was born in 1920, one of eleven children raised in a three-room house with no indoor plumbing or electricity, in the mountains of West Virginia. I knew her life as a child had been much different than the one I'd had, but I wasn't aware of exactly how until I read her story. It tells of how they gathered holly to decorate with, and pine to burn in the fire on Christmas Eve. The children hung their black stockings on the back of a chair in view of the fireplace where Santa would be sure to see them. On Christmas morning, each stocking would be filled with five sticks of candy, an apple, a sweet cake, on rare occasions an orange and sometimes a handful of peanuts in the shell. Christmas breakfast was wheat pone bread, blackberries, pork and honey and butter, and their Dad always said a long prayer before they could go to the table. For Christmas dinner, they had chicken dumplings. At the end of the day, before going to bed, all the children would sit in a circle around the fireplace as their dad read scripture and had the "night prayer". Those simple Christmases were special memories for my grandmother. She could have told me the stories, but having them in writing is so much better. This gift has been even more special to me because my grandmother passed away the following summer, making this the last Christmas gift I would ever receive from her. Sometimes the simplest gifts are the ones we value most.

Holiday Memories

Phyllis Peters
Three Rivers, MI

Every Christmas, thoughts of my many blessings flood my mind and I recall the holidays of my youth. Times were tough then; the Depression had taken homes and jobs. People in our small Michigan village felt helpless. But due to good fortune, financial disaster had bypassed my grandmother, who had been successful in business ventures. She and my aunt made sure I was provided for very well. But the best gift Grandma Reed gave me was her wonderful spirit of giving. Grandma told me, at age six, "We are so blessed we must share with others less fortunate." As I helped Grandma pack baskets of food and hand them out to families who needed them, I sensed a feeling of warmth as the recipients expressed their thanks. Grandma also advised, "It's important to do for others not only at Christmas, but all year long."

I carried Grandma's legacy with me, and when I had a family of my own, I passed the trend of giving by example. Together, our family collects food and essentials to give to the needy throughout the year and my children have begun performing acts of kindness on their own. My alert daughter saw smoke coming from a building, reported it, and saved the life of an elderly gentleman. I was so proud of her actions when his family praised Connie's concern for others. My grandchildren and great-grandchildren have been taught by their parents and the gift of giving continues to live on in my family. Every Christmas, four generations of my family seek out a project for the needy in our area, carrying on the tradition begun by Grandma so many years ago. Because of Grandma, we have the Christmas spirit in our hearts all year long.

Far away family members would love to see an updated picture of your family. Round everyone up around the tree, including family pets, dress in festive sweaters, put the kids in holiday striped pajamas...have fun!

Mary Tollefson
Marshfield, WI

At the time I am writing this, our daughter, Abby, is two years old. She was given to us as a gift on St. Nick's day. Abby, you see is a twin. We lost our other special twin, but still have the joy of Abby. This is a very special memory for us. Abby's daddy, Mike, and I decided not to wrap Abby's dolly this year. Instead, we sat her under the Christmas tree so that she would be the first thing Abby would see when she woke up that Christmas morning. Early Christmas morning, we lay in bed waiting for Abby to wake up. The electric coffee maker had started dripping and we could smell the sweet aroma of coffee drifting into our bedroom. We waited for what seemed to be forever for her to wake up.

Finally, we heard the little shuffle of feet down the hallway. Now, as a parent, we all know that familiar sound that "footy pajamas" make when scuffed along a carpet. She headed right to the Christmas tree where her dolly was sitting, awaiting her arrival. We next heard her run down the hallway to our room and crawl into bed, clutching her already very much loved new dolly. Ordinarily we would think she would want to open her other presents, but she nestled tightly between us and calmly sighed, "He came," closed her eyes with a smile and fell back asleep. My husband and I looked at each other and smiled almost in disappointment, but yet very happy knowing we were only postponing our excitement of watching her open her other presents for a short while. Meanwhile, we laid back smelling the fresh coffee and thinking about those home-made blueberry muffins awaiting us when little Abby did awake.

Enjoy the peacefulness of winter. As the days grow short, light candles, stoke the fire and settle in to dream.

Holiday Memories

Rosee Boehme
Boise, ID

Christmas was always such an enchanting time when I was a little girl. Since I am almost 70 years old, that time was during the Depression. My mother raised three children by herself, so you can imagine how scarce money was for anything but the barest essentials. Somehow my mother always managed to smuggle a scraggly Christmas tree to our third story apartment. I always believed that Santa brought and decorated the tree. I never saw it until Christmas morning, and what a thrill it was. We didn't have many presents, but we did have love, which is the true meaning of Christmas. My greatest pleasure was to lie under, and gaze up through the lighted tree. This was so special since we lived in Brooklyn, with no grass or trees. Even though we live where there are plenty of trees now, my grandchildren and I still keep up my tradition and enjoy looking up at the lights through the tree!

"It's not the gift, but the thought, that counts."

-Anonymous

Wendy Lee Paffenroth
Pine Island, NY

Going back a few years to when my children were in elementary school, I decided to do something different with our Christmas tree. We always cut a real tree from their father's hunting camp or our aunt's Christmas grove of pines. On this particular year, I had been watching holiday craft shows and one in particular told how to make "snow" for your tree, using soap flakes, water and an electric beater. So, after the tree was trimmed, lights on, cranberries and popcorn strung, I set to work whipping up the snow. It came out the consistency of dairy topping and you dripped it over the branches. It was beautiful, and the tree looked like it had fresh snowfall on it. The only trouble was that the house smelled like detergent. No matter how many pine candles I burned, how many pine-scented items I set out, or cans of pine-scented bathroom spray I used, the house still smelled like laundry. For three weeks it smelled like that. All the ornaments that had the "snow" on them had to be cleaned. I spent a long time with the ornaments and a toothbrush trying to get the "snow" off. To this day, I still find "snow" on ornaments. We had to throw out the lights, too! Even though they worked the next year, that smell was still there. So, before I try to "improve" on our Christmas again, I'll do a bit more research!

In Colonial Williamsburg the yule log is burned and a sprig of holly is tossed on the blazing log, in the old English custom, to burn up the troubles of the past year.

Marlene M. McGovern, Brunswick, ME

Holiday Memories

Peggy Dannehl
Grand Island, NE

My youngest sister was born in January, so needless to say, the Christmas before was hard on my mother. We lived on a farm with a lot of work and very little money. A few days before Christmas, my mother's aunt brought over lots and lots of homemade, beautifully decorated Christmas cookies! Wow! My mother lined a bottom drawer in the cupboard so we could get a cookie whenever we wanted. Those are still the best cookies I ever ate.

Sandra Pinkerton
White Hall, IL

When I was about four years old, I remember at Christmas time my parents ordered a crate of oranges from the Sears and Roebuck catalog, and they came in on the train that passed through our small town of Hillview. That was in 1946 and people in our community were not affluent. The best memory I have of those days is the smell of the oranges, the wooden crate with the wire hooks, and the beautiful green tissue paper that each orange was wrapped in. To this day, I still eat and love oranges and my favorite color has always been green. We weren't rich, but our family and friends have memories that money can't buy.

Index

Index

stockings golden hillsides Christmas carols tailgate parties fudge honeybees candles on the tree stuffing twinkling lights family gatherings snowflakes pumpkins warm fuzzy sweaters hot mulled cider snowforts Indian corn pot bellied stoves candle lit windows stockings golden hillsides Christmas carols tailgate parties fudge honeybees candles on the tree stuffing twinkling lights family gatherings snowflakes pumpkins warm fuzzy sweaters hot mulled cider snowforts Indian corn pot bellied stoves candle lit windows hot mulled cider snowforts Indian corn pot bellied stoves candle lit windows stockings golden hillsides Christmas carols tailgate parties fudge honeybees candles on the tree stuffing twinkling lights family gatherings snowflakes pumpkins warm fuzzy sweaters

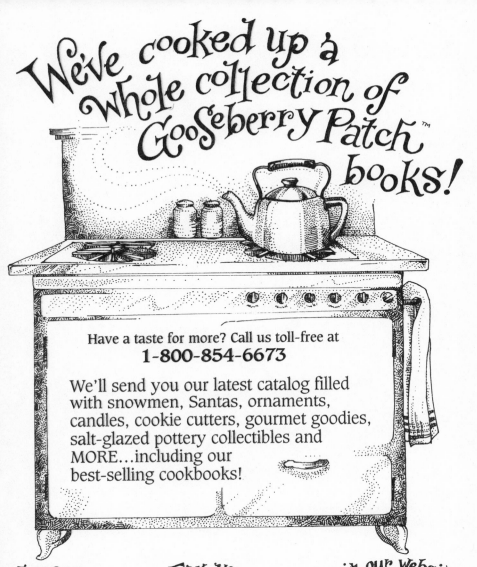

We've cooked up a whole collection of Gooseberry Patch™ books!

Have a taste for more? Call us toll-free at
1-800-854-6673

We'll send you our latest catalog filled with snowmen, Santas, ornaments, candles, cookie cutters, gourmet goodies, salt-glazed pottery collectibles and MORE...including our best-selling cookbooks!

Fax us: 1·740·363·7225

Visit our Website: www.gooseberrypatch.com

Send us your favorite recipe!

*and the memory that makes it special for you!** We're putting together a brand new **Gooseberry Patch** cookbook, and you're invited to participate. If we select your recipe, your name will appear right along with it...and you'll receive a FREE copy of the book! Mail to:

Vickie & Jo Ann
Gooseberry Patch, Dept. BOOK
P.O. Box 190
Delaware, Ohio 43015

*Please help us by including the number of servings and all other necessary information!

stockings golden hillsides Christmas carols tailgate parties fudge honeybees candles on the tree stuffing twinkling lights family gatherings snowflakes pumpkins ... ers hot mulled cider snowforts Indian corn pot bellied stoves candle lit windows

Prospect Free Library
0001500135932